Perspectives

Andy Hopkins

Series developed by Andy Hopkins
and Chris Tribble

Longman

Longman Group UK Limited,
Longman House, Burnt Mill, Harlow,
Essex CM20 2JE, England
and Associated Companies throughout the world.

First published 1989

Set in 9/11 Palatino roman

Printed in Italy
by G. Canale & C. S.p.A. - Turin

ISBN 0 582 01665 7

Acknowledgements
We are indebted to the following for permission to
reproduce copyright material:
Associated Book Publishers (UK) Ltd for an adapted extract
from *The Book of Heroic Failures* by Stephen Pile (pub.
Routledge & Kegan Paul Ltd); the editor for an extract from
the article 'Blunder caused air crash' in the *Evening Standard*,
3.8.88; Independent Television Publications Ltd for a letter
from the *TV Times*, 30.1.88; Mirror Group Newspapers Ltd
for extracts from *The Sunday Mirror* 24.1.88 (c) The Daily
Mirror Newspapers Ltd; the author, Peter Murtagh and The
Guardian for his article from *The Guardian*, 6.1.88.

We are grateful to the following for their permission to
reproduce copyright illustrative material:
British Airways for page 43; Brother Office Equipment for
page 42; Camera press for pages 35, 66 top centre, 66 middle
centre and 66 middle right; J Allan Cash for pages 39, 66 top
right, 66 bottom left and 66 bottom centre; Keystone
Collection for page 50; Olympus Cameras for page 13;
Paperchase for page 32; Picturepoint for pages 66 middle left
and 66 bottom right; Rex Features for pages 21, 53 and 66 top
left; Royal County of Berkshire for page 41; D. C. Thomson
& Co Ltd. 1987 for page 64 and Janine Wiedel for page 16.

We regret that we are unable to trace the copyright holder of
the article and photograph on page 58 and would welcome
any information enabling us to do so.

The illustrations are by Ray Burrows, Kathy Baxendale and
Hardlines.

Contents

Map of the book

Unit	Title	Topic	Writing skills
1	Thinking About Writing	Awareness-raising	• Developing awareness of types of error • Identifying personal writing needs
2	Organising Writing: Using Linking Words and Phrases	Reference	• Developing awareness of text organisation • Linking clauses and sentences
3	Improving Your Writing	Reference	• Developing awareness of approaches to writing • Improving texts: editing and rewriting
4	Writing a Letter to a Friend	Keeping in touch	• Recognising and applying conventions of informal letters: organisation and layout; common phrases for opening and closing
5	Writing Letters of Complaint	Complaining	• Recognising and applying conventions of formal letters: organisation and layout; opening and closing
6	Applying for a Course of Study	Writing letters asking for information/Filling in an application form	• Recognising and applying conventions • Form-filling
7	Writing a Personal Description	Job application	• Recognising and responding to reader needs • Paragraphing
8	Taking Notes	Computers/Social services	• Developing awareness of different methods of note-taking • Identifying main and subsidiary points

Unit	Title	Topic	Writing skills
9	Writing Instructions	Instructions and directions	• Recognising and responding to reader needs
10	Writing a Newspaper Report	Crime	• Recognising conventions of newspaper reports • Writing headlines
11	Writing a Biography	Famous people	• Organisation and layout • Paragraphing
12	Writing a Report Describing Change	Change	• Generating ideas • Logical grouping of ideas into paragraphs
13	Reporting the Results of a Survey	Surveys	• Examining reader expectations • Organisation and layout • Paragraphing • Presenting a list
14	Creating a Mood	Story-telling	• Recognising and applying story structure • Generating ideas • Planning writing • Creating a mood
15	Writing an Essay: Approaching the Task	A woman's place. . .	• Analysing essay questions • Brainstorming • Organising ideas • Developing a writing plan • Drafting • Reviewing and editing • Redrafting
16	Writing an Essay: Patterns of Organisation	Military service	• Recognising and applying conventions of organisation and layout

Southampton Technical College
Department of General &
Continuing Education

To the teacher

INTRODUCTION

This book aims to develop in learners the ability to write effectively in English for a range of useful purposes. The materials focus on two central areas:

- the organisational conventions of particular text types (what the 'product' is like)
- the skills a writer needs to approach and see through particular writing tasks (what is involved in the writing 'process')

While *process* and *product* are useful terms for thinking about language use, it seems obvious that good materials should simultaneously encourage learners to become better writers by focusing on general techniques useful to text creation and evaluation, as well as provide them with organisational frameworks which make explicit the sociocultural and linguistic conventions that are part of the knowledge base called on by native speakers when they write. This book tries to apply what we know about how people write and how texts are structured in a way which is helpful to learners.

The materials have been designed so that they may be used either in the classroom with a teacher or by students working alone – with some monitoring by a teacher. This design feature allows the teacher a great deal of flexibility in organising the balance between what is done as a group in the classroom and what is done by individuals or small groups of students working independently outside the classroom. Suggested answers to all exercises are given in the Key at the back of the book.

CONTENTS

A detailed list of the book's contents is provided on pages 4–5. However, it is worth pointing out that the first three units differ in purpose and content from the remaining units. Unit 1 is a general awareness-raising unit which requires learners to reflect upon different types of writing and different types of written error. Unit 2 reviews and introduces a range of linking devices while Unit 3 encourages the learner to reflect on the writing process itself. Unit 3 is an important unit in that it provides a reference list of features against which the student checks first drafts. Learners are referred to this checklist throughout the book.

Each of the remaining units deals with a different text type. The text types covered in this book are ones that commonly feature in the major international EFL examinations at Intermediate and Upper-Intermediate level, particularly Cambridge First Certificate, RSA CUEFL, and Oxford Delegacy. The units on essay, biography and report writing also provide some practice for students preparing for the ELTS examination. However, the principal criterion for the selection of text types is their value to the learner in terms of their usefulness in the real world. Some text types have been included not because they are often required of a non-native speaker but because they provide a suitable vehicle for focusing on certain process skills.

It is not necessary to work through the book in the order presented. However, you are strongly advised to cover Units 1, 2 and 3 before looking at units in the remainder of the book. This is particularly important if you intend to use the book as part of a self-study scheme.

UNIT METHODOLOGY

FEATURE	PURPOSE
Discussion	• To bring in learners' knowledge
	• To predict prior to reading activity
Stimulus and Model Text	• To exhibit relation between stimulus and target text type
	• To provide model text for analysis – to derive explicit organisational framework
Enabling Activities for Main Writing Task	• To work on information structure and language features
	• To work on text generation techniques
Main Writing Task (Drafting)	• To go through a process to generate a product similar to the parallel model text
Follow-up	• To exchange texts with partner
1 Comparing Texts with Partner and Key	• To evaluate own and partner's text against Key text
2 Improving Text using Checklist in Unit 3	• To improve own text

It is important to note that the Key is an integral part of each unit. It is not only an 'Answer' section but also contains model texts with which the learner is invited to compare his or her efforts at various stages in the unit.

MANAGING THE WRITING CLASS

The writing class provides a number of management problems for the teacher. We have to decide whether or not extended writing will take place *in* the class – the advantage being that we can monitor the process; the disadvantage being that writers work at varying speeds – or *outside* the class – which is administratively preferable but prevents us from being near the learner at the moment that problems actually occur. These are possible ways of managing the writing class:

	IN CLASS	OUTSIDE CLASS	IN CLASS (Follow-up)
1	Work through whole unit and begin main writing task	Complete main writing task (first draft)	Rewrite text
2	Work through unit but do not begin main writing task	Do main writing task	Rewrite text
3	Work through unit but do not begin main writing task	Do main writing task Compare, edit and rewrite	Tutorials from time to time to look at first and final drafts

Of course there are many other options for organising the programme. You may wish the learners to work through the unit in a self-study mode and to use the class time as a series of *writing workshops* in which you devote time to individuals and groups working together.

MARKING WRITING

a *When to mark and reasons for marking*
According to the methodology implied by these materials, the teacher should not see the 'final' written work until it has been drafted and rewritten. The purposes of marking at this stage are:

- to encourage and give praise for achievements
- to ensure that the learner has understood and effectively gone through a process of planning, drafting, comparing and rewriting
- to ensure that the learner has got to grips with the objectives of the unit – particularly the organisational conventions of the text type and its linguistic features

b *Establishing a marking code*
It is essential that you establish a marking code early on. It is worth writing this down on a sheet of paper and giving a copy to each of the students, who can then utilise it if they wish when editing their own texts.

When marking a 'final' text try not to cover the page with indications of errors. Be positive and point out only those errors which seriously affect communication and which you can say something constructive about.

c *Writing Skills profile*
A profile sheet is given after the Introduction. You may wish to use this from time to time with the student to give an idea of progress. It is a good idea to complete this with the student in a tutorial session and use it as a basis for discussion. Alternatively, you could ask students to complete it for each other or to use it at intervals to evaluate their own writing.

To the student

This book can be used in the classroom or for self-study. Suggested answers to all the exercises are given in the Key at the back of the book. If you are working alone, complete Units 1, 2 and 3 first. When you have done these units you may choose to do any of the remaining units in whichever order you wish.

After completing the final writing task in each unit you should follow the procedures in the checklist in Unit 3 for improving your writing. Edit and rewrite your text before comparing it with the model in the Key. When you have produced your final text, show it to a teacher or if you do not have access to a teacher, to someone who speaks and writes good English. If possible, find a partner to work with and compare and discuss your texts. Remember that the model texts in the Key are *suggested* versions. Others are possible! Good luck!

Writing profile

Use this 'Writing profile' to give feedback to students *after* they have produced their second draft.

Communicative quality
1 Communicates what is intended clearly and effectively.
2 Communicates intentions quite well.
3 Communicates intentions adequately.
4 Does not communicate intentions adequately.
5 Fails completely to communicate intentions.

Logical organisation
1 Information and ideas extremely well-organised.
2 Good organisational structure.
3 Organisational structure evident with some breakdowns.
4 Difficult to identify logical structure.
5 No logical structure evident.

Layout and presentation
1 Extremely well-presented. Shows complete familiarity with conventions.
2 Reasonably well-presented; a few minor problems with conventions.
3 Acceptably presented but needs more familiarisation with conventions.
4 Some serious gaps in familiarity with conventions.
5 Fundamental lack of familiarity with conventions.

Grammar
1 Wide range and excellent control of appropriate grammatical structures.
2 Effective use of a good range of grammatical structures.
3 Adequate range and control of grammatical structures.
4 Limited range and poor control of grammatical structures.
5 Extremely limited range and control of grammatical structures.

Vocabulary
1 Wide range and excellent control of appropriate vocabulary.
2 Effective use of a good range of vocabulary.
3 Adequate range of fairly appropriate vocabulary.
4 Limited range of vocabulary.
5 Extremely limited range of vocabulary.

Handwriting, punctuation and spelling
1 No faults.
2 Occasional faults.
3 Adequate but needs improvement.
4 Significant weaknesses.
5 Little knowledge of or ability to handle the basic conventions.

Thinking About Writing

Introduction

For many people, mastering writing is the most difficult aspect of learning a foreign language. This unit looks at the different kinds of difficulties people have and some of the sorts of mistakes people make when writing in English.

Some common mistakes

1 Look at the short texts below. They contain a number of mistakes to do with spelling, punctuation, grammatical use and organisation. Work with your partner to fill in the grid, then rewrite each correctly.

a) I'm afraid I not can to come tomorrow.
b) He said she would probably arrive in january.
c) Are you going home during the summer, this year!

d) Please keep quite in the library.
e)

```
Mrs H E John,
London NW1 4NS,
England.
18,Baker Street,
```

TEXT	SPELLING	PUNCTUATION	GRAMMAR	ORGANISATION
a)				
b)				
c)				
d)				
e)				

Write the correct answers here.

a) _____

b) _____

c) _____

d) _____

e)

Another kind of mistake

2 Now look at these pairs of texts below. One of each pair is acceptable but the other has something wrong with it. Work with your partner and decide:

- which texts are *un*acceptable
- what is wrong with the 'bad' texts

LETTER A

```
                          72 The Street
                          Morley
                          Norfolk  NR18 9AF

                          26/9/88


The Manager
Midland Bank
Norwich

Dear Sir,

I need some money urgently.   Please send
£2,000 by tomorrow.

          Love

               Ted
```

LETTER B

```
                          72 The Street
                          Morley
                          Norfolk  NR18 9AF

                          26/9/88


The Manager
Midland Bank
Norwich

Dear Sir,

I am writing to ask if it would be
possible to take out a loan.

I have recently moved to a new house
which has no central heating.   The
estimated cost of installing a complete
system is £2,000.   I wonder if you
could let me know if the bank would
consider lending me that amount.

If I need to complete an application
form I would be grateful if you could
send me one as soon as possible.

Yours faithfully,



E.G.Thomas
```

TELEX A

```
ATTENTION: P THOMAS. MANAGER. TECHNICAL SERVICES
          BD LTD. 42 GEORGE STREET. COLINDALE. LONDON NW9
FROM:
          ARTHUR DENNISON. EAST-WEST CO. PO BOX 86.
          CONNAUGHT STREET. HONG KONG
I HOPE YOU ARE FEELING WELL.   I AM WRITING TO ASK IF YOU ARE ABLE TO
PROVIDE SERVICE IN HONG KONG FOR THE M462 COLOUR PHOTOCOPIER
PRODUCED BY YOUR COMPANY.   IF THE ANSWER IS YES I WOULD BE MOST
GRATEFUL IF YOU WOULD SEND AN ESTIMATE FOR THE COST OF A ONE YEAR
SERVICE CONTRACT AS SOON AS POSSIBLE.

YOUR SINCERELY

ARTHUR DENNISON
```

TELEX B

```
Document Number :  71

ATTENTION P THOMAS. MANAGER, TECHNICAL SERVICES

FROM       ARTHUR DENNISON. EAST-WEST CO.

RE         COLOUR PHOTOCOPIER M462

PLEASE ADVISE IF SERVICE IS AVAILABLE ON THE ABOVE
MACHINE IN HONG KONG.   IF SO. PLEASE SEND DETAILS
OF AGENT AND ESTIMATED COST OF ONE YEAR SERVICE
CONTRACT.

REGARDS
```

Points to consider when writing

3 Check the Key to make sure you have completed exercise 2 correctly. You will now realise that writers make mistakes not only of punctuation, spelling, grammar and organisation but also of **appropriacy**. To write appropriately it is important to consider the following points carefully:

- Our **purpose** for writing
- The **audience** – the person or people we are writing to
- The **type of text** chosen (letter, telex, report, etc.)

Look at these four texts. Work with your partner to fill in the grid at the top of the next page. Then discuss with your group the features (words, grammar, pictures, etc) that helped you to decide.

A

It was a lovely morning in Greendale. The sun was shining. The birds were singing. Where was Postman Pat? It was long past his time to be up and on his way, but his curtains were closed and his van stood outside. All was silent and still. Then ... the door opened and Pat looked out. He looked sleepily at his watch. "Oh dear, is it that time?"

Postman Pat's Difficult Day, Andre Deutsche, 1982.

B

Sitter target

Now that I am 14, my parents have finally allowed me to baby-sit for my three sisters, who are 12, 10 and eight. But my grandmother strongly disapproves, saying that by law I cannot be left responsible for younger children until I am 16. Is this true? I fear she is purposely misinforming my parents to weaken their trust in me.
Julia
Chichester
West Sussex

C

'Blunder' caused air crash

HUMAN error was responsible for the shooting down of an airliner over the Gulf last month, according to a U.S. Navy report.

Iran Air Flight 655 was shot down by the U.S. cruiser Vincennes, killing all 290 people on board.

The American TV network ABC, quoting the report, said Navy investigators concluded that the ship's sophisticated radar system was not to blame.

"The report concludes that human error was primarily responsible for the disaster," ABC said last night.

The ship's commander, Captain Will Rogers, ordered a missile attack on the plane after he was told it was descending toward the ship with the high speed of an attacking fighter plane.

But computer records show the Aegis radar missile targeting system accurately determined the Iranian plane was climbing.

D

1 **Load the camera** (see page 7). Make sure the battery has been properly inserted and that the camera back is closed tightly.

2 **Set ASA Film Speed** (see page 12).

3 **Advance the film until the figure "1" appears in the exposure counter window** (see page 9).

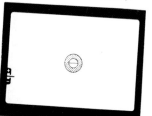

4 **Look through the viewfinder. Compose and focus. Set the proper exposure** (see pages 13, 14, 15).

5 **Take the picture** (see page 19). Hold the camera steady and release the shutter with a slow, steady pressure.

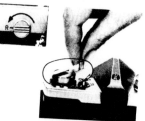

6 **After the entire film has been exposed, rewind the film back into the cartridge** (see page 10).

TEXT	PURPOSE	AUDIENCE	TEXT TYPE
A	Entertainment	children	story
B			
C			
D			

Your reasons for writing

4 This book offers help with the development of writing skills in the context of a number of **text types** in English. Look at the list below and decide which are likely to be valuable to you in your use of English both **now** and in the **future**. Fill in the table yourself then discuss with your group.

TEXT TYPE	NOW	FUTURE
Letters to friends Letters asking for information Telexes Poems Short stories Letters of application Letters of complaint Reports Newspaper articles Forms Argumentative essays Descriptive essays Notes (from reading)		

Organising Your Writing: Using Linking Words and Phrases

1 Put these sentences in the right order to form an amusing story.

The Worst Bank Robbers

a) A few minutes later they returned and announced that they were going to rob the bank.

b) They had to be helped free by the staff and, after thanking everyone, left the building.

c) In August 1975 three men were on their way to rob a bank at Rothesay in Scotland, when they got stuck in a revolving door.

d) When at first they demanded £5,000, the head cashier laughed at them, thinking it was a practical joke.

e) The gang leader then reduced his demand first to £500 and then to £50 and finally 50 pence.

f) By this time, the cashier could hardly contain his laughter.

g) The other two made their getaway, but got trapped in the revolving door a second time, desperately pushing the wrong way.

h) Then one of the men jumped over the counter but slipped on the floor and hurt his foot.

2 We use many different kinds of knowledge to help us to complete tasks such as that in exercise 1. These include **knowledge of language** and **knowledge of the world**.

2.1 Knowledge of the world
Because you knew the story was supposed to be funny you were probably expecting it to be organised in the following way:

BACKGROUND SITUATION → EVENTS → OUTCOME

This knowledge helped you to identify the first and probably the last sentence. Think of funny stories or jokes you know in your own language. Tell them to each other. Are they organised in this way?

2.2 Knowledge of language
You also used your knowledge of English to help you put the sentences in the right order.

a) Words and phrases which tell you the **timing** or **sequence** of events are particularly important. Look at the words in exercise 1. Write down all the words and phrases which give you an idea of the **sequence** of events.
a few minutes later,

_____

(For more work on **Time Linkers** see *Outlines*, Unit 2, in this series.)

3 Read the sentences at the top of the next page. The words in italics are linking words but they are not **Time Linkers**. What are they? What kind of relationship is there between the parts of the sentences that they link together?

- The match this afternoon is cancelled *because of* bad weather.
- There has been no rain *so* the crops can't grow.
- *Since* there is a baggage handlers' strike there are no flights today.
- People are in danger *as a result of* radiation leaks from nuclear power stations.
- Smoking is dangerous *therefore* it shouldn't be allowed in public places.

Linkers that connect Cause and Effect/ Consequence

4 The linkers in exercise 3 are used when we want to indicate **Cause-Effect** relationships. Look at the sentences again and decide which is the **Cause** and which the **Effect** or **Consequence**. Write (C) or (E) above the appropriate part of each sentence.

4.1 Writing task: Linkers of cause and effect
The text below has some parts missing. Rewrite it in full inserting the words in boxes at appropriate places.

Millions facing starvation as crops fail

Once again the rains have failed to come in time to Ethiopia. Millions of people are facing starvation.

Emergency food and medical supplies are being sent through international relief organisations and stockpiled at ports. However, transportation of these supplies to distant areas remains an almost impossible problem.

More than fifty per cent of the lorries used in the last relief operation two years ago are damaged beyond repair.

because of the lack of good roads and the continuing civil war.

so the relief organisations are desperately seeking international help to send in supplies by plane.

As a result, the crops planted last year have not grown.

5 Study these sentences then complete each gap below with one of the **Cause-Effect Linkers**. There are many possible answers. Think of *all* the words that can fit.

a) The match was cancelled _____ it was raining heavily.

b) The trains were running late. _____ I missed the start of the meeting.

c) He is a vegetarian _____ he can't eat the main course.

d) _____ she had parked her car dangerously, the police towed it away.

e) None of the people interviewed for the job were suitable. _____ it had to be advertised again.

| consequently   so   because   as a result |
| as   since   therefore |

Other linkers

6 Read the text below and look carefully at the linking words and phrases in italics. Put each linker into the correct box.

TIME/SEQUENCE	COMPARING AND CONTRASTING	GIVING EXAMPLES	EXPLAINING

In Britain, the majority of children attend state schools. *However*, in the last ten years the number of private schools has increased steadily. What are the main differences between private and state secondary schools?

5   *Firstly*, there is the size of classes. In private schools the average class size is about 15, *while* the figure is closer to 35 in state schools. *Secondly*, the family background of the children tends to be different. *Whereas* children at private schools generally come from quite well-off families, those in state schools come from a wide

10   variety of social and cultural backgrounds. *For example*, a recent survey of children in a typical state secondary school in London showed that children in the same class came from families from widely different income groups, religious and racial backgrounds. *By contrast*, private schools have very little social or cultural mix.

15   Another important difference concerns facilities. There is no doubt that the bigger private schools have better facilities – *such as* science laboratories, computer centres, sports facilities – than many state schools.

    Many people believe that parents – if they are willing and able to

20   pay – should have the right to send their children to private schools. I don't agree. *What I mean by this is* that all children have the right to the same high quality of education regardless of their parents' income.

Using linkers: Comparing and contrasting/ Giving examples/ Explaining what you mean

7.1 Comparing and contrasting

The most useful linkers of comparison and contrast are *while* and *whereas*. Find them in the text above. Notice that they can occur at the **beginning** of a sentence or **between** two clauses. Join these pairs of sentences.

a) 95% of children attend state schools. 5% attend private schools.
b) George is taller than Peter. Peter can run faster than George.

7.2 Explaining what you mean

Look at this pair of sentences.

> In my opinion military service should not be compulsory but some kind of *social* service should. That is, young people should be required either to do military service or work in the community.

The linker *that is* is used to show that the second sentence **explains** or **expands** the first sentence. Other phrases which you could use include *in other words*, *what I mean by this (is). . .*

7.3 Giving examples

Look at this sentence.

> All young people should be required either to do military service or to work with disadvantaged people in the community – for example, those in hospitals, old people's homes, special schools.

We can replace *for example* by *for instance*. We could begin a new sentence and write *Some examples of this (kind of community service) are. . . .*

Rewrite these pairs of sentences using appropriate linkers from 7.2 and 7.3. Combine them into one sentence where necessary.

a) I don't agree that military service teaches a young person useful skills. Learning how to kill is not a useful skill.
b) I can think of lots of reasons why compulsory military service is a good idea. It allows you to meet people from different backgrounds.
c) If military service is to be compulsory it should be compulsory for everyone. Women should also be obliged to do military service.

Improving Your Writing

For most types of writing there are conventional models which help you to **organise** your writing. These models are provided in the remaining units of this book. However, knowledge of the organisational conventions is not sufficient to make you a good writer. Good writers also go through particular procedures **before** writing as well as **during** and **after** writing a first draft.

Approaching writing

1 Read what these people have to say about how they approach a writing task and fill in the grid at the top of the next page.

1.1 Student – Writing essays

The first thing I do is to read the question carefully. Then I make notes on the main points of the essay – this helps me to establish
5   what reading I need to do in order to answer the question. I often discuss the essay question with a friend to make sure I've understood what needs to be done. As I read I
10   make quite detailed notes and then organise the points in the order they will be presented. After that I write the body of the essay and then the conclusion and
15   introduction. When I've completed the first draft I read it through to check that I've included all the points I want to make, and reread the question to make sure I've
20   answered it properly. I usually find I have to rephrase bits of the essay to make it clear what my argument is. I also often have to change the order of some of the points to make
25   the argument more logical. If possible I ask a friend to read what I've written to see if it makes sense. Finally, I check my spelling and grammar and write my final draft. I
30   use a dictionary quite a lot.

1.2 Businessperson – Writing letters and reports

The most important point to remember about writing in a business context is that the people you are writing to are
5   busy and want to be able to find information quickly and easily. I write to get things done. A good letter or report should therefore be clear
10   and concise, and of course, the information must be accurate and complete. I write straight on to a word processor so I don't make
15   notes before writing. In fact the company I work for has a strict policy for how reports should be presented so I don't need to think too
20   much about layout. I try to put myself in the position of the reader and only include the information that he or she will find relevant. I write
25   the separate sections and then assemble the report and print it out. I read it through to see if it makes sense and is well organised
30   and clear. Then I read it again to check for accuracy, punctuation and grammar. After that I edit the first draft. I've got a program in
35   my word processor that checks my spelling – which is fortunate because I'm not a good speller! If possible I get a colleague to look at the
40   report before I hand it in.

1.3 Novelist

**Different writers work in different ways. I have a rough idea of a plot and the kinds of characters I'm going to include
5   before I write but I find that the real ideas come to me while I'm actually writing. I spend far more time drafting and revising than I do on planning – I wrote six
10   drafts for my last novel before I was happy. I spend a lot of time thinking about individual words and phrases that convey the particular mood or feeling I'm
15   trying to create. If I make errors in spelling and punctuation they are usually typing errors and are picked up by my editor so I don't systematically check for that
20   kind of thing – that's the job of the proofreader.**

a) Work with your partner and write notes about what each of the people above actually do at the following stages:

	STUDENT	BUSINESSPERSON	NOVELIST
Before writing			
While writing first draft			
After writing first draft			

b) One of the writers above mentions the importance of thinking about **who** you are writing for. Work with your partner and fill in the grid below with information about **who** each writer is writing for and what you think their readers' reasons for reading are.

	WHO ARE THEY WRITING FOR?	WHAT ARE THEIR READERS' REASONS FOR READING?
Student		
Businessperson		
Novelist		

c) What do YOU do when you have to write an essay in your own language? Work with your partner and make notes about how you plan, write and revise your work.

2 When you have written a first draft it is not enough to check spelling, punctuation and grammar. Here is a useful procedure for improving your first draft. This checklist is important and you will be referred to it in all the following units.

Checklist for improving first drafts

First reading
Check that information in your text makes sense
- Is it laid out well – according to the models shown in each unit?
- Have you included all the information that is relevant to your reader?
- Have you *excluded* irrelevant information?
- Is the information presented in a clear and logical sequence? (see Unit 2)

Second reading
Check that words and phrases are appropriate
- Have you used any words or phrases that are too formal/informal for your purpose?
- Can you replace commonly-used 'general' words by words which convey a more particular and accurate meaning?
- Do the words and phrases adequately describe the *strength* of what you want to say?

Check spelling, punctuation and grammar
- Have you made any spelling errors?
- Have you used punctuation appropriately?
- Have you made any grammatical errors?

Writing task

3 This task focuses on the points in the checklist under *FIRST READING* above. Rewrite the letter so that it excludes irrelevant information and includes all relevant information in a logical order.

14 Doris Road
Norwich
26 August 1988

The Manager
Theatre Royal
Norwich

Dear Sir / Madam,

I hope you can find my bag. I left it in the Theatre last week when I came to see my daughter who was appearing in 'The Boyfriend' – It was such a good production, though I thought the tickets were a bit expensive!

Please let me know if it has been handed in. The bag is black, made of soft leather and has the initials BJ on the front.

Yours faithfully,
Barbara.

- Is it laid out well?
  - address/date etc.
  - beginning and ending
  - the main body of the letter
- Is this information relevant or irrelevant?
- Is the information presented in a clear and logical sequence?
  - what information should you give first?

Now rewrite the letter.

Writing task

4 This task focuses on the use of appropriate words and phrases under the *SECOND READING* section of the checklist. The words in italics in the text below are either inappropriate in some way or are too general and could be replaced by more particular words. Work with your partner and, using a dictionary to help you, decide on more appropriate or exact words/phrases.

THATCHER, Margaret Hilda (1925–   )

Margaret Roberts was born in Grantham, Lincolnshire in 1925. She (1) *got* interested in politics as a child through her father who was (2) *two times* mayor of Grantham. At Somerville College, Oxford she (3) *did* chemistry and was president of the University Conservative Association. In 1949 she stood for parliament but (4) *did not get in*. She married Denis Thatcher in 1951 and (5) *had* twins, a boy and a girl, two years later. She was elected to parliament in 1959. After holding (6) *a lot of* important posts in the Conservative Governments of 1960–64 and 1970–74, she became party leader and in 1979 Prime Minister. She (7) *got* a reputation for toughness and was named 'Iron Lady' by the Soviets.

Writing task

5 This task focuses on errors of spelling, punctuation and grammar. Work with your partner and rewrite the text below in a more appropriate way.

My name is Natalie Hirsch. I am twenty years old and I study Grafic disegn in my country. One of things I like must is stay with children. If I don't study Grafic disegn I hope that I had study to be a teacher because I like to much to play with people. I have a lot of pacient with children. I will like to get a job in London to look after children. I thing that is going to be a very good expereince if I find the job I think to stay here about three years.

spelling/punctuation
spelling/grammar
grammar
spelling/grammar
spelling/vocabulary
grammar
spelling/grammar
spelling/grammar
grammar

Writing a Letter to a Friend

Have you got any friends you write to in English – perhaps people you met while you were on holiday or while you were on a course somewhere? Maybe you have a pen friend? This unit looks at the language of letters which have a very important purpose – keeping in touch with friends! In this sort of letter we usually tell friends our latest news – about things we've done, places we've visited, people we've met.

Parts of letters

1 Look at these sentences and phrases. Some are quite formal and others are informal. Which are you likely to find in letters to friends? Discuss with your partner and put a tick (✔) next to those you think you *would* find:

a) How're things?
b) See you soon!
c) I am writing to inform you of my change of address
d) Take care!
e) Yours sincerely
f) Yours faithfully
g) Look forward to seeing you in August!
h) I refer to your letter dated July 28th
i) Thanks for your recent letter
j) It was so nice to hear from you

2 Now look at the sentences again. In most letters they are likely to appear at the beginnings and endings – but which ones appear where? Discuss with your partner and finish the lists below.

BEGINNINGS	ENDINGS
I am writing to inform you of my change of address	Yours faithfully
_____	_____
_____	_____
_____	_____
_____	_____

3 Look at this list of the functions of parts of letters to friends. Then read the letter at the top of the next page and match the list to the different parts of the letter labelled a – j.

1 Write your address _____
2 Write the date _____
3 Express pleasure at receiving your friend's letter _____
4 Start the letter _____
5 Say goodbye _____
6 Bring the letter to a close _____
7 Give your news _____
8 Ask some questions _____
9 Respond to your friend's news/questions _____
10 Apologise for not writing _____

72,Hurst Park Avenue
Cambridge CB4 1AF

b 23/2/88

c Dear Jack,

d Thanks for your letter - it was such a surprise to hear from you after all this time!

e I must apologise for not keeping in touch. I'm afraid I'm such a terrible letter writer!

f I'm so glad to hear you and Eileen are well and happy and that the kids are getting on well in their new school.

g Since I last saw you my life has changed quite radically. I'm married now, I've changed my job and we've just moved house! I won't go into it all now - it's much too long a story!

h How about meeting up soon? Now that you're back in Britain perhaps we could all get together one weekend? How do you feel about coming up to Cambridge at Easter? Let me know if you can come. There's plenty of room for you all here.

i By the way, Barbara sends her love. Hope to see you soon.

j All the best,

Andy

Improving writing

4 Look at the letter below from Karsten to his friend Dick. There are quite a few mistakes and oddities which have been picked out. Work with your partner and try to improve the letter.

NORREGADE 77,
6200 YARDE,
DENMARK

28/10/88

Dear Dick,

It was so nice to get your letter. I want to write you a long time but I'm not good to keep in touch!   } Grammar

I'm glad you're enjoying your new job. I think it is very exciting, isn't it? Since I've seen you last time I am   Grammar
doing a lot of different thing. After I left London I   Grammar
traveled to paris to met my friend, then we went to   Spelling/Grammar/Punctuation
south France to found work for a month picking grapes.   Grammar
It was a hard work but the pay was quite well. At the   Grammar/Grammar
end in September I returned to my home to start a   Grammar
course in Hotel management. I'm enjoying the course
but I'm looking forward for the Christmas holidays!   Grammar

What are you doing on Christmas? How about come to   Grammar/Grammar
visit us here - there's plenty of spaces. Think about it   Grammar
and tell me soon.

My mother sends her love. Hope to see you at Christmas.
Goodbye,
Karsten

Inappropriate ending

5 Read the letter below which is Dick's reply to Karsten. When you have read it once do exercises 5.1, 5.2 and 5.3.

48, Cherry Road
Cambridge
CB2 2QX

15.11.88

Dear Karsten,

Thanks for your recent letter – it was good to hear from you. Forgive me for not replying sooner.

Thank you also for the Christmas invitation – I'd love to come and am fairly sure I'll be able to make it.

Guess who I saw last week? Sara! Do you remember her? I'm sure you do. We went out for a meal and had a great time. She's studying at the Royal College of Music and seems to be enjoying it very much. She sends her love.

What arrangements do we need to make for Christmas? My holiday starts on December 19th and I have to be back by January 2nd. When shall I come to Denmark? How do you suggest I travel?

Hoping to hear from you soon,
Dick.

5.1 Thanking someone

Here are some phrases you can use to thank people. Some express thanks strongly, others express thanks in a fairly neutral way. Put a tick (✔) next to the expressions you think are strong.

Thank you very much . . . .
I'm so grateful . . .
Thanks . . .
I can't thank you enough . . .
I'm grateful . . .

5.2 Describing how you feel about something you've done

> . . . we had a *great* time

Look at these words. Work with a dictionary and decide which express positive feelings (good) and which express negative feelings (bad).

	GOOD	BAD
great		
wonderful		
awful		
amazing		
horrible		
terrible		
fantastic		
lovely		
marvellous		
pleasant		
disastrous		
appalling		
depressing		
nice		

5.3 Making suggestions

Dick asks Karsten to make suggestions about how to travel to Denmark. We could use any of these phrases:

- *Why don't you* take the ferry?
- *How about* flying?
- *The best way to* come is by train

Now use these phrases to make suggestions in the following situations:

- a friend wants to take a holiday abroad but doesn't know where to go
- a friend needs to get hold of some money quickly . . . any suggestions?
- you're in a restaurant with a friend who isn't familiar with food from your country

Writing task

6 Imagine you have received a letter like Dick's from a friend of yours. Write back making arrangements for your friend to visit you. Suggest some dates, how he/she should travel, and what you might do together during the visit.

After writing

7 a) Refer to the checklist in Unit 3 and try to improve your text.
   b) Exchange texts with your partner and make suggestions for improvement.
   c) Compare your text with the one suggested in the Key.

Extension task

8 Why not find a pen pal who you can write to in English. Your teacher may be able to help you.

Writing Letters of Complaint

Organising writing

When you write a letter of complaint it is important to make your complaint **effectively**. To do this you should be:

BRIEF   CLEAR   ORGANISED

1 Look at this letter of complaint to a shop manager. The words in the boxes below describe the different parts of the letter. Put them in the correct place on the right. The first one is done for you.

| ADDRESS OF THE PERSON YOU ARE WRITING TO | DATE | YOUR NAME | DEAR _____ |

| ACTION REQUIRED | MAIN REASON FOR WRITING | BACKGROUND INFORMATION 1 |

| COMPLAINT | BACKGROUND INFORMATION 2 | ENDING |

```
                                    48 Hill Road      1
                                    London SE1 4PN

                                    26 November 1987  2

3   The Manager
    Design Shop
    14 Abbey Gate
    London NW3 5AP

4   Dear Sir/Madam

    I am writing to complain about a hair drier bought in your
    shop last Saturday and about the treatment I received when
5   I tried to return it a few days later.

6   I bought the hair drier – a RAVLON 405 – on Wednesday 22nd
    November. The first time I tried to use it the handle
    became extremely hot and within a few minutes part of the
    plastic casing began to melt. I turned it off
7   immediately and returned it with the receipt to your shop
    on Saturday.

    I explained the situation to one of the assistant and
    asked for my money back but was told I had to speak to
8   you. Unfortunately you were not available that day so I
    am writing instead.

    I enclose the hair drier and a copy of the original
9   receipt. Please send me a full refund as soon as possible.

10  Yours faithfully
    Sabrina Sari
11  Sabrina Sari (Ms)
```

1 _Your address_
2 _____
3 _____
4 _____
5 _____
6 _____
7 _____
8 _____
9 _____
10 _____
11 _____

2 Work with your partner and decide on answers to these questions.

a) How does the layout of this letter differ from a letter to a friend?
b) Why does the writer use 'Dear Sir/Madam'?
c) The writer uses 'Yours faithfully' to end the letter. She could also have used 'Yours truly'. Could she have used 'Yours sincerely'? Why/why not?
d) The writer signs herself as _Ms_. What does this mean? What about Miss, Mrs and Mr?

Language focus

3.1 Stating your main reason for writing

You should state your main reason for writing in the **first** paragraph of the letter. Use the situations below to write first sentences like the one in the letter:

Example: You bought a shirt last Monday.

I am writing to complain about the shirt I bought from your shop last Monday.

a) You bought a TV last Thursday
b) You bought a watch on Friday
c) You hired a car from a company on Tuesday
d) You had a meal in a restaurant on Sunday

3.2 Giving background information and describing a problem

In the **second** paragraph you will usually need to give some background information – this may involve explaining how you discovered the problem. This paragraph is usually written in the **past**.

a) Rewrite the following in the past tense to describe how you discovered something was wrong with a TV you bought last Thursday.

> I / buy / TV / your shop / Thursday 23rd November / but / when turn on / not work. / check / plug / but / not the problem.

b) Rewrite this to describe the problems you had when you hired a car.

> I / hire / car / your company / Tuesday 18th February. / drive / London / catch / plane. / On the way / have / puncture. / When / take out / spare tyre / find / is / flat / and / no tools. / try / phone you / no answer. / miss / plane.

c) Here are some situations and problems. Match them to make complete sentences.

SITUATION	PROBLEM
When I put on the shirt	I found it was flat
When I took out the spare tyre	it started to get hot
As soon as I turned it on	the heel fell off
The first time I wore them	I discovered it was torn

d) Now make sentences which begin with the words and phrases in italics and which describe a problem. Here are some problems:

Example: You buy a computer which doesn't work

When I switched it on the keyboard began to get hot.

- You buy a loaf of bread and find some glass in it
- You buy a chair which falls apart when you sit on it

3.3 Requesting action 1

The **final** paragraph in a letter of complaint usually contains a request for action of some sort. Requests for action can be very strong, or quite mild. Are the phrases below strong (1) or quite mild (2). Write a number 1 – 2 next to each.

a) I demand that you refund my money immediately. ☐
b) I hope you can send me a replacement as soon as possible. ☐
c) If you do not refund my money immediately I will contact my solicitor. ☐
d) Please replace the faulty radio as soon as you can. ☐
e) I would be grateful if you could send me a refund soon. ☐
f) I will come into the shop on Saturday to collect a new one. ☐

3.4 Requesting action 2

Ms Sari asks the manager to send her a *refund*.
Look at these phrases. They describe different kinds of action you might request. Which one from the list is similar in meaning to each of the phrases in italics in the sentences below.

give me a refund	give me a replacement	give me an apology

give me an explanation	give me a discount

a) I am writing to ask you to *send my money back*.
b) I feel you should *give me a reduction in the price*.
c) Please *send me a new one*.
d) You must *tell me what happened*.
e) I demand that you *say sorry*.

Organising writing

4 Reorganise this letter. Use the model in exercise 1 to help you.

> 12th February 1988
>
> The Manager
> Savoy Restaurant
> 76 High Street
> Liverpool
>
> 42 Long Road
> Liverpool
>
> I took a group of business friends to the restaurant because I had heard that the food and the standard of service was excellent.
>
> I feel that at the very least you owe my guests and me an apology and await an answer from you.
> I am writing to complain about a meal I had in the Savoy Restaurant last Friday evening.
> However, when we arrived at the restaurant we found that no reservation had been made although I had confirmed it by phone the day before. After waiting for a table for over an hour we were kept waiting a further hour before we were served. When the food finally arrived the vegetables were cold and the plates were dirty. When I complained to the waiter he became rude. I was disgusted by the treatment we received and shall certainly never eat there again.
> Yours faithfully,
> Colin Thomas,
>
> Dear Sir/Madam

Writing task: Punctuation

5 Study the letter at the beginning of this unit carefully. Note that CAPITAL LETTERS are used for **names** (of people, streets, towns/cities, months, companies) and for '*Yours*' in the ending to the letter. They are of course also used **at the beginning of sentences**. Rewrite the letter below inserting capital letters, commas and full stops where appropriate.

24 Albert Road
Manchester

15 April 1988

The Manager
College Bookshop
26 Stone Square
Manchester

Dear Sir/Madam,

I am writing to complain about a book I bought in your shop on saturday morning, The name of the book was the 'Guide to British Birds' I was in a hurry so I didnt examine it very carefully before I paid for it. When I got home I sat down to have a look at it and found to my surprise that a number of pages were missing.

I enclose the book with a copy of my receipt. Could you please send me a replacement as soon as possible.

Yours faithfully,

John Stephenson

Writing task

6 *Either* You have bought a new record from a record shop called Pete's Place. When you try to play the record you find that it is badly scratched. Write a letter to the manager asking for your money back or for a new record. The address of the shop is: 212 Oxford Street, London.

Or Write a letter of complaint about something that you **really** want to complain about!

DON'T FORGET!

- Be brief, clear and organised.
- Follow the model in exercise 4 on page 28.
- Check your spelling, grammar, punctuation and layout.

After writing

7 a) Go through your letter using the checklist in Unit 3. Now improve it.
  b) Exchange texts with your partner. Check his/hers against the same checklist.
  c) Compare your letter with the suggested version in the Key.

Extension task

8 Imagine you have been on a holiday which you booked through a travel company. There have been all kinds of problems.

a) Work with a partner and make a list of all the different things that could go wrong on holiday.
b) Now one of you take the role of the travel agent and the other the person with the complaints. Act out the conversation.
c) Now choose some of the main problems and write a letter of complaint to the travel company.

Applying for a Course of Study

You may find that you want to apply for a place at a school, college or university in an English-speaking country. This unit looks at the writing tasks associated with making applications of this kind.

Discussion

1 Think about these questions and discuss them with your group.

a) What are the advantages and disadvantages of studying overseas?
b) Do you think you would face difficulties other than those associated with studying in a foreign language? What kinds of difficulties might they be?
c) How do you feel about others coming to your country to study?

2 Look at this advertisement for courses at the University of Gwent which appeared in an Educational Supplement.

University of Gwent

The University will be offering a limited number of postgraduate courses specially arranged for overseas students, commencing in October 1990. These courses will be taught over two years and will include a component aimed at raising students' abilities to use English language in an academic context.

Courses leading to the degree of Master of Arts are offered in the following subjects:

English and American Studies   Linguistics   History
International Studies

For further details and an application form write to:
The Registrar, University of Gwent, Newtown, Gwent, South Wales, UK.

Writing a letter asking for more information

3.1
Stavros Giorgiou, a student from Cyprus wrote a letter to the university asking for more information. Fill in the missing words in the letter below then rearrange the paragraphs. Write the rearranged letter in full.

Yours _____,

Stavros Giorgiou

The _____
University of Gwent
Newtown
Gwent
South Wales,UK

I am particularly interested in the MA _____ in International Studies.

I saw your recent _____ in an Educational Supplement concerning postgraduate

courses for _____ students.

Could you please send me full _____ and an application _____.

September 23 1989

18 Famagusta Street
Nicosia
Cyprus

Dear Sir/Madam,

Organisation

4 If you completed exercise 3 correctly you will see that the organisation of a letter asking for more information is like this.

```
                        Your address
                        Date

Dear . . . ,

  ┌─────────────────────────────────────┐
  │ PARA 1  Refer to the advertisement  │
  └─────────────────────────────────────┘

  ┌─────────────────────────────────────┐
  │ PARA 2  Refer to the part of the    │
  │ advertisement that you are interested│
  │ in                                   │
  └─────────────────────────────────────┘

  ┌─────────────────────────────────────┐
  │ PARA 3  Ask for more information     │
  └─────────────────────────────────────┘

Yours ...,

Your name
```

5 Look at the advertisement below which appeared in a newspaper. Write a letter asking for information and an application form.

REGENTS COLLEGE

Study in the heart of London this summer. Four and eight week courses available in the following areas:

American Studies
English Literature
Computer Studies
Drama

Write for more information and an application form to: **The Registrar, Regents College, Inner Circle, Regents Park, London NW1 4NS**

Filling in an application form

6 Stavros sent his letter to the University of Gwent and received an information booklet and an application form. Study the form on page 33 and work through the exercises below.

6.1 Understanding the form: Vocabulary development
Work with your partner and consult a dictionary if you wish to find words or phrases in the application form which mean the same as:

a) capital printed letters _____

b) family name _____

c) previous _____

d) native language _____

Find a word which means the **opposite** of:

e) temporary _____

6.2 Useful information for filling in forms
Courses towards **degrees** in Britain are either at Bachelor or Master level. Most degrees are for *Arts* or *Science* subjects though some other subjects such as *Law*, *Music* and *Business Administration* have special titles. Look at the abbreviations below. Which degrees do you think they stand for?

Example: BA *Bachelor of Arts*

a) MA _____   d) MSc _____

b) BSc _____   e) LLB _____

c) BMus_____   f) MBA_____

6.3 Filling in the form

Most of the form is straightforward and requires information about you and the course you wish to apply for. Only one part requires you to do any connected writing – *REASONS FOR WISHING TO TAKE THE COURSE*. In this part you should write why you are attracted to this course rather than another and why you want to study in Britain. Look back at the advertisement for courses in Regents College in exercise 5 and write two sentences giving your reasons beginning with these words:

I am interested in taking the course because _____

_____

I want to study in Britain _____

_____

Now *either* fill in the form opposite with information about yourself *or* use the information below about Stavros.

> Stavros Giorgiou was born in Cyprus on July 28 1967. He's single and lives with his parents in Nicosia. He went to the International School from the age of 11 and left at 18 with GCE Advanced levels in Geography (B) History (A) and Economics (A). After that he went to Athens University from 1986–89 to study for a BA degree in Business Administration. He left the university with an average grade of A. He wants to study International Studies because he hopes to become a diplomat and is interested in the course at the University of Gwent because he has heard from a friend that the course is good.

Extension tasks

7 You can use the same letter format as that shown in exercise 4 for writing for more information in response to job advertisements. Choose one of the job advertisements below and write a letter.

PAPERCHASE

We are the leading name in fashionable stationery, greeting cards, giftwrapping etc, and we are soon coming to BROMLEY *and* KINGSTON.

We are now looking for the right people to fill the following positions:

MANAGER
We need a highly motivated, enthusiastic person to take responsibility for the day to day running of the new store, achievement of sales budget is a priority as is effectively managing a team of staff to ensure high standards of customer service and display.

ASSISTANT MANAGER
To fill this position we are looking for someone with flair and enthusiasm and the ability to merchandise and sell our exciting range of fashionable stationery goods. As your main duty is to support the Manager in the running of this busy store, some supervisory experience is preferred.

SALES ASSISTANTS
As most of the time you'll be dealing face to face with the customer, enthusiasm and confidence are vital in this challenging role. The ability to form part of a team is essential.

We are also looking for an ASSISTANT MANAGER to work in our busy OXFORD STREET branch, where the ability to organise and motivate is essential.

If you are interested in any of these positions, and would like to join Paperchase then please write

Vivien Aiton, Paperchase Products Ltd, 213 Tottenham Court Road, London, W1P 9AF.

Please include your day time telephone number.

SELECTION LIMITED, Tie Rack

Tie Racks' largest franchise has IMMEDIATE VACANCIES in its WEST END, GUILDFORD and CROYDON branches for

MANAGERS
SALESPERSONS
PART-TIMERS

WE WILL PAY TOP SALARIES FOR THE RIGHT PEOPLE.

TO GET ON OUR NEW YEAR'S HONOURS LIST
Please phone Paul on 437 3870 or write for application form to: 93a Regent Street London, W1R 7TE.

University College of Gwent

Registration for a higher degree or research course

SURNAME *(Block letters)*	FORMER SURNAME *(If applicable)*

FIRST NAMES *(In full)*	MARITAL STATUS M = Married S = Single ☐	SEX M = Male F = Female ☐

DATE OF BIRTH ___ ___ ___ day month year	NATIONALITY	MOTHER TONGUE

PERMANENT HOME ADDRESS Telephone number:	COUNTRY *(If Overseas)* OR COUNTY *(If U.K.)*

ADDRESS FOR CORRESPONDENCE DURING THIS APPLICATION Telephone number:	IF YOU HAVE ATTENDED THE SCHOOL BEFORE STATE DATES AND SUBJECT(S) TAKEN

COURSE PROPOSED 1. Title of degree: 2. Subject: 3. Full-time/Part-time: 4. Starting date:	REASONS FOR WISHING TO TAKE THE COURSE

PREVIOUS EDUCATION
 (i) Schools attended since age of 11:

(ii) School leaving certificate obtained *(If GCE Advanced Level, give the grades)*:

(iii) Universities attended with dates	Degree	Main Subject	Class or Grade	Date
(iv) University at which you are presently enrolled:			Date of examination:	

Writing a Personal Description

There are a lot of situations when we need to write descriptions of ourselves – for example: when we apply for jobs; when we write to penfriends overseas; when we need to introduce ourselves by letter to someone. Can you think of any others?

Discussion

1 Look at this advertisement and discuss the questions below.

SUMMER IN LONDON

Professional English family requires young person 18–25 to look after two children (7 and 9) from July to September. Own comfortable room and all meals provided. Generous salary and plenty of time off. Please write or phone for an application form to Mrs P Young,
14 Redcliff Gardens,
London NW3 4FJ
Tel: 01-032-6754

---

a) What sort of family is a *professional* family? Which of these are 'professional' people?

doctor	teacher	factory worker
Schreiber typist	mechanic	engineer
lawyer	nurse	train driver

b) Does the job sound attractive? Why?
c) If you were Mrs P Young what would you want to know about the people applying for the job? Make a list with your partner.

Vocabulary expansion

2 What kind of **qualities** do you think Mrs Young is looking for?

Here is a list of words used to describe people's characters. Decide with your partner which you think are **good** qualities for the job advertised by Mrs Young. Use a dictionary to help you decide.

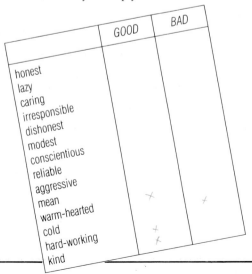

	GOOD	BAD
honest		
lazy		
caring		
irresponsible		
dishonest		
modest		
conscientious		
reliable		
aggressive	✗	✗
mean		
warm-hearted		
cold	✗	
hard-working	✗	
kind		

3 An Italian girl, Gina Montesi, decided to apply for the job. This is the application form she sent to Mrs Young. How does the information Gina gives about herself compare with the list you made in exercise 1c) on page 34.

Family Name: MONTESI	First Name: GINA

Address: Via Felice Casati 20
20124 Milano

Tel. 010 - 39 - 2 - 2043867

Date of birth: 10/10/68   Nationality: Italian   Sex: F

Experience of looking after children:

1987 - Summer job with family in Rome. 3 children 5, 7 and 11

Please tell us about yourself and why you would like the job.

As you can see, I'm from Milan in Northern Italy. I live at home with my parents, two sisters and brother. As the oldest child I have always helped with looking after my younger sisters and brother.

I'm in my second year at Milan University where I'm studying English and Business Studies. I hope to finish next year and would like to find a job with a large company where my English will be useful.

I have lots of hobbies and interests. I enjoy sports like tennis, squash, horse-riding and - of course - skiing, but also spend time reading, going to the theatre and the opera. I play the piano - my friends tell me I play well but I don't think I'm very good.

I'm interested in the job because it would provide the opportunity to improve my English while doing something I enjoy very much - working with children. I feel that I am responsible, trustworthy and hardworking. I am also quite cheerful and I think I have a good sense of humour - which is essential for anyone working with children!

Being tentative

4 When we write we sometimes want to sound **certain** about something. At other times we may want to sound **tentative**. People are likely to be tentative when saying or writing about positive aspects of their character.

Example:

I *think* I have a good sense of humour.

Can you find other places in Gina's letter where she uses words that suggest tentativeness?

Getting the right tone

5 Here is another application that Mrs Young received for the job from a Spanish girl. Read it carefully and decide which of the comments below you agree with. Work with your partner.

> I'm from Madrid in Spain. I have two young brothers and sisters so I know what to do with children.
> I want to come to England to learn English better and do a lot of sightseeing. I do not mind living in London and I think your house is near the centre. I have some friends in London so they could come and visit me.
> Please tell me exactly how much the pay is and when my holidays will be. Also is it necessary to work on Saturdays and Sundays because I want to travel around Britain.

The letter:

	AGREE	DISAGREE

a) . . describes her personal qualities in great detail
b) . . suggests she is very interested in children
c) . . suggests that her main reason for wanting to come to England is to do the job
d) . . does not contain enough information about herself
e) . . is too short
f) . . is rude

Now rewrite the letter. Try to improve it. Make it more **tentative.**

Organising information

6 Gina's letter is organised to provide answers to certain questions she thinks Mrs Young wants to ask. Look at the questions below and put them in the order that they are answered in Gina's letter. Write the questions in the paragraph boxes at the top of the next page.

a) What are your plans/hopes?
b) What do you do?
c) Where do you live?
d) What qualities do you have which make you suitable for the job?
e) What interests do you have?
f) Why do you want the job?
g) How big is your family?

PARAGRAPH 1	PARAGRAPH 2
1 2	1 2

PARAGRAPH 3	PARAGRAPH 4
1	1 2

Writing task

7 Imagine you are replying to Mrs Young's advertisement. Tell her about yourself and why you are interested in the job.

BEFORE YOU WRITE

Think about these questions:

- Who are you writing to?
- What does the person you are writing to want to know?
- How do you want to appear to your reader? How can your choice of words help?

WHILE YOU WRITE

Use the paragraph organisation in exercise 6 above to structure your writing.

After writing

8 a) When you have written your text, look at it carefully. Study the checklist in Unit 3 and try to improve what you have written.
 b) Exchange texts with your partner. Point out any improvements you think can be made.
 c) Compare your text with the one suggested in the Key.

Extension tasks

9 We can describe ourselves in different ways depending on our **purpose** for writing and what we think the **reader** is interested in. Gina's description of herself in exercise 2 concentrates on her abilities with *children*.

 a) Write a description of yourself that would be useful if you were applying for a summer job in a shop where you would be responsible for large sums of money.
 b) Write a description of yourself that would be useful if you were applying for a job which involved leading a team of people – for example, being in charge of a group of workers on a summer camp, or being the captain of a team, or the representative of your school/college.

Taking Notes

You may need to take notes while you are listening to people speaking – for example in a lecture – or while you are reading. This unit concentrates on taking notes from **written** sources.

Discussion

1 Work with your partner and decide on answers to these questions. Then discuss your answers with the rest of the group.

a) Why do people take notes? Think of as many reasons as you can.
b) How do you take notes in your own language? Describe what you do when you have to take notes from a book to prepare for writing an essay.
c) Do you use abbreviations and symbols in your notes? Write down as many as you can think of.

Abbreviations and symbols

2 Here are some abbreviations and symbols commonly used by English speakers. Match them with the words and phrases given.

ABBREVIATIONS

e.g.	a) Take note
etc.	b) that is
i.e.	c) for example
NB	d) namely
viz.	e) compare with
cf.	f) and so on

SYMBOLS

=	g) causes
≠	h) therefore
+	i) because
∴	j) is not the same as
∵	k) also, and
→	l) results from
←	m) is the same as
>	n) more than
<	o) less than

3 Look at these notes written by a student. Using the list of abbreviations and symbols above to help you, rewrite the sentences.

1. 25% road accidents ← drunk drivers in 1986
2. 60% British people took holidays abroad in 1988 cf. 1981 – 42%. Most pop. destinations – Mediterranean e.g. Greece, Turkey, Spain

4 Now you try to write these sentences in note form. If you already use abbreviations and symbols of your own, use them here. Otherwise use the abbreviations and symbols suggested in exercise 2.

a) Heat causes ice to melt.
b) The standard of living in Britain is lower today than it was 10 years ago.
c) Computers are used much more widely today than 10 years ago because they are much cheaper.
d) Children learn foreign languages more easily than adults. Therefore foreign languages should be taught in primary schools.

Organising writing: notes

5 Look at the text below entitled *The Computer Revolution*. As you read it decide on a **question** that each of the paragraphs answers and write the questions in the boxes on the right. The first question for paragraph 1 is done for you.

The Computer Revolution

In the past ten years the world has witnessed a computer revolution. There is now hardly any aspect of everyday life that does not bring us into contact with computers, whether it be in shopping at the supermarket, or using them at work, school, or
5   play. Computers have become a vital tool for governments, the armed forces, banks, businesses and industries.

    The first electronic computer, built over 30 years ago, took up the space of a large basement room. Today, the essence of a computer of equal calculating power can be built onto a small
10   sliver of the material silicon smaller than a postage stamp. Such micro-miniaturization of electronic circuits has led to small, cheap, powerful and reliable computers for the home and office.

    The computer's great advantage over human beings is its
15   ability to store vast amounts of information and the incredible speed at which it can work. In the time that it takes to read this page, a computer can perform millions of operations. This makes it ideal for repetitive, detailed work, such as keeping company accounts, analyzing statistics, and monitoring
20   production in factories.

    But although they work at such speed, it is important to remember that computers are not "intelligent." They are only machines that perform the tasks they have been instructed to undertake. Without instructions and information supplied by
25   their operators, computers are no more intelligent than the metal and plastic of which they are made.

Computer: The Inside Story, Aladdin Books, 1983.

a) How widely are computers used today compared with 10 years ago?

b)

c)

d)

6 Notes should be **clear** and **relevant**. That is, they should only contain information which is **useful** to your purpose, and you must be able to **understand** them when you look at them again after a few days.

Look at these three sets of notes. Which one do you think best summarises the main facts of the text *The Computer Revolution*?

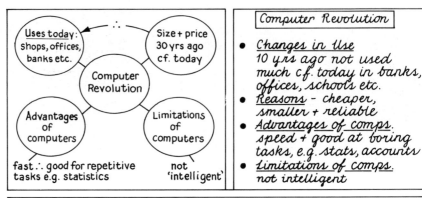

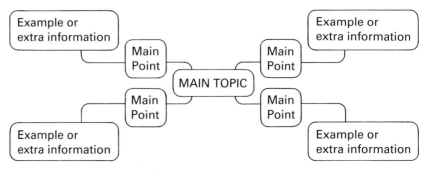

Make notes here about the main ways in which the sets of notes differ from each other.

_____

_____

_____

_____

7 Many people find the graphic form of notes shown in B above very helpful. They can be written quickly and reconstructed and recalled quite easily. They are organised like this:

Example or extra information — Main Point — MAIN TOPIC — Main Point — Example or extra information

Example or extra information — Main Point — MAIN TOPIC — Main Point — Example or extra information

Writing task

8 In Britain, certain local services are provided by the *county council*. Every year each council sends a leaflet to every home to tell people how their money will be spent in the coming year. Read the leaflet carefully and make notes on the main areas of expenditure for **this year**. Organise your notes as shown in exercise 7 on page 40.

YOUR SERVICES

Royal County of BERKSHIRE

EDUCATION

The education of school children, students in colleges, Adult Education, the Youth Service and the Careers Service. THIS YEAR sees an expansion of nursery education, a new primary school in Bracknell, and improvements to schools across the county. More money is to be spent on books and equipment, computer facilities, support for GCSE, and on a new youth and community centre in Slough. *7,611 teachers and lecturers, 1,731 support staff in schools and colleges, 2,190 caretakers, cleaners, groundsmen and school meals staff and 254 administrative and support staff are working to provide you with a quality education service.*

SOCIAL SERVICES

The welfare, care and protection of children, the elderly, the handicapped and others in the community who are in need. THIS YEAR a new day centre for physically handicapped people is to be built in Wokingham, extra facilities are being provided for people with mental handicaps, a network of family centres is being developed in Reading and an extra £1m will be spent to improve and extend services. *Care is provided by 3,084 staff working directly with clients and 263 support staff.*

HIGHWAYS & PLANNING

Improving and maintaining roads, bridges and street lighting, the co-ordination of public transport, traffic management schemes and overall planning for the county. THIS YEAR sees further work on Reading's Inner Distribution Road, contributions to a new railway station in Bracknell and environmental improvements across the county. *533 engineers, roadmen and planners are employed to maintain and enhance your environment.*

FIRE & RESCUE

The fighting and prevention of fires and the provision of a rescue service. THIS YEAR there are to be more full-time fire fighters, new vehicles and provision for a new fire station in South Reading. *523 firemen and support staff are employed to protect you.*

LIBRARIES

Lending, reference services and support for the Arts. THIS YEAR sees improved staffing levels, new libraries for Ascot and Theale and an extension for Britwell library. *You are served by 348 librarians and support staff.*

Extension task

9 A good test of the effectiveness of your notes is to try to reconstruct the main points of the text in **written form** from your notes. Do this now without looking at the text in exercise 8 then compare your final text with the original.

FINAL NOTE

There is no **right way** to take notes. Experiment with different methods of note taking until you find a way that is right for **you**. Do try to become familiar with a range of abbreviations and symbols which **you** understand. Notes that you make from a particular text will depend upon your **purpose** for reading the text in the first place. Remember that you should **only** include information that is relevant to **your** purpose.

Writing Instructions

The most important point about instructions is that their main purpose is to convey **information**. Good written instructions are **clear** and **concise**. They contain only information which is necessary in order to carry out a particular task.

1 Look at these instructions from a computer printer manual on how to remove a ribbon. The pictures are in the correct order but the sentences are not.

a) Match the sentences at the top of the next page with the pictures below and then reorder the sentences so that they make sense.

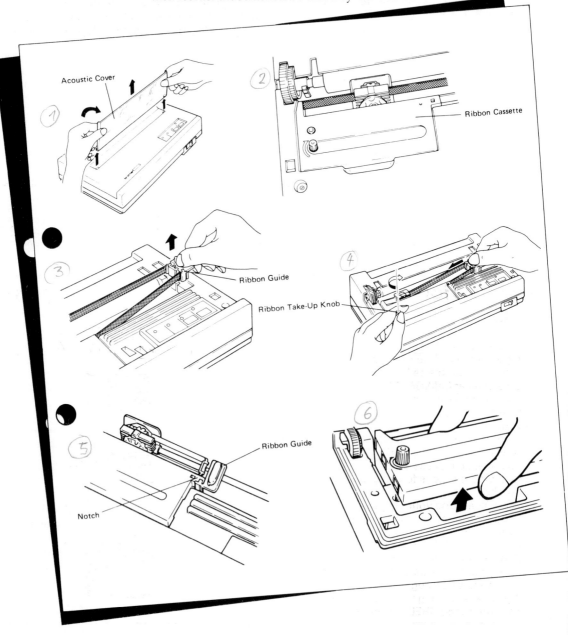

i) First lift the acoustic <u>cover up</u> and forward, then remove it.

ii) Put the ribbon guide <u>into</u> the notch on the right side of the cassette.

iii) Turn the ribbon take-up knob clockwise with the left hand and wind up the ribbon until it stops.

iv) Move the print head to the centre of the ribbon cassette.

v) Lift up the ribbon guide with the right hand.

vi) Finally lift up the ribbon cassette at the centre and remove it from the printer.

b) Read the text above again and underline all the **Time Linkers.**

c) The instructions above contain a number of references to 'it'. Read each sentence carefully and write down what 'it' refers to in each case.

SENTENCE i) _____

SENTENCE iii) _____

SENTENCE vi) _____

d) i) Underline all the verbs in each sentence. What do you notice about their **form**? How would you make them **negative**?

ii) Why do the verbs have no subject? Who do we understand as the subject?

Reformulation

2 Look at these instructions to passengers on arrival at Heathrow Airport. They are not clear or concise enough. They contain too many words. Rewrite them so that they contain the features of the instructions in exercise 1. Remember that many people who need to understand these instructions are likely to have some difficulty with English language.

Instructions for British Airways Passengers arriving at London Heathrow Airport.

- Please will you <u>follow</u> the ARRIVALS signs carefully. You can see them hanging from the ceiling.
- On arrival at IMMIGRATION you will need to show your passport and any health documents you are carrying with you.
- Next you should proceed to the ARRIVALS BAGGAGE RECLAIM AREA. You'll be able to see where to go by following the signs for your flight number.
- When collecting your luggage it's a good idea to check to make sure it's yours – many bags look alike.
- Next go to CUSTOMS. You can go through one of two channels. If you have goods to declare please be kind enough to go through the RED channel. If you have nothing to declare you can go through the GREEN channel.

Writing task

3 Look at the pictures below which give instructions for what to do if you have a pan fire with cooking oil in your kitchen. Write a paragraph of continuous writing explaining the procedures.

REMEMBER!

- Use **Time Linkers**
- Use the **Imperative** form
- Do NOT use subject pronouns (e.g. *you*)
- Be clear and concise, and include only **useful** information
- You are writing for people who may have difficulty with English

Begin like this:

If oil catches fire in a frying pan. . . .

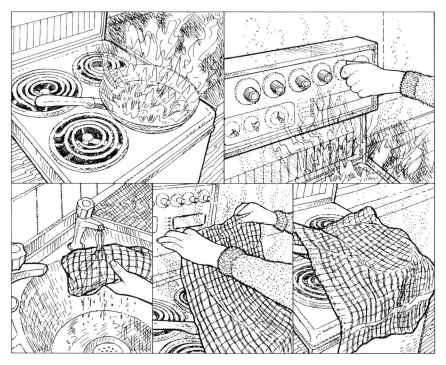

Instructions: Giving directions

4 a) Look at these two sets of spoken directions. Which do you think is better? Why?

i) Go straight ahead (er) . . . then take the first turning on your right and the second on the left. After that it's the third right (er) . . . first left, first right and it's in front of you.

ii) Go straight on to the traffic lights then turn right. Go along that road and take the second on the left at the station. This takes you on to Broad Street. Continue along Broad Street and take the third turning on the right – there's a school on the corner. After that it's first left and first right. You can't miss it.

When we give directions to others, whether in speech or writing, it is important to give the listener or reader some markers to check their progress along the way. The computer printer text does not do this, but the Heathrow airport one does.

b) This is a map of Heathrow Airport. Read the instructions on the left and mark the position of the underground station and the Control Tower.

To get to the underground station from Terminal Three Arrivals, go straight ahead along the front of Terminal Three Departures until you come to Car Park Two. Follow the road to the left and then take the first turning on the right between the Control Tower and the side of Car Park Two. Go around the Control Tower past Terminal Two and the station is on the corner on your left opposite the Queen's Building.

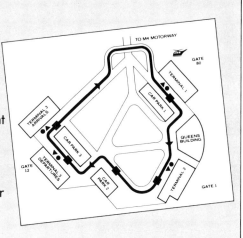

Writing task

5 Now look at this map. You want a friend to meet you at the White Horse Hotel. Leave a note describing how to get there from the station.

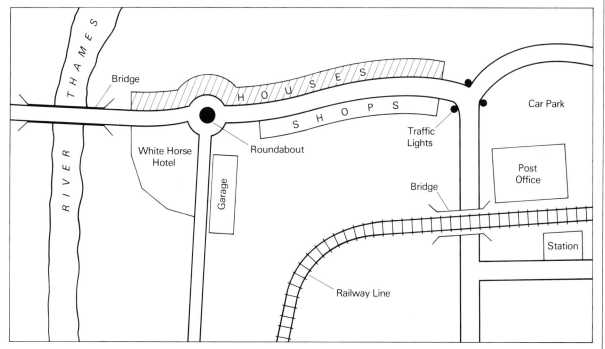

After writing

6 a) Try to improve what you have written by working through the checklist in Unit 3.
b) Exchange texts with your partner and work through the same checklist.
c) Compare your final text with the one suggested in the Key.

Extension activity

7 Think of a game you know – perhaps a card game – and write instructions for how to play it.

Writing a Newspaper Report

Newspaper reports differ from other kinds of writing in important ways.

Organising writing

1 Look at the list below and tick (✔) those features which are present in the newspaper report headed *MASKED MAN ROBS RENT COLLECTOR*.

Headline	Details of crime
Name of writer	Description of criminal
Information about the	Name of criminal
kind of crime committed	Appeal for witnesses

Man with hammer robs rent collector

A COUNCIL rent collector was attacked and robbed in Townhill on Monday.

The official from Swansea Borough Council was collecting cash in Neath Road just before 9am when he was robbed.

Police say the robber, brandishing a club hammer, forced the victim to hand over his cash bag and a portable telephone so that he could not raise the alarm.

The bag contained £560 in cash.

The robber is described as 18–25 years old, slim build and about six feet tall. He was wearing a dark jacket, blue jeans and dark-coloured work boots.

His face was masked by a balaclava or hood and a blue scarf pulled across the mouth.

Detectives hunting the robber have released a photograph of the type of cashbag and telephone stolen in the attack. A police spokesman said, 'We are hoping that either someone will remember seeing the offender running off carrying these items, or know where they were later dumped.'

The Swansea police spokesman added, 'We are very anxious to trace any witnesses to the attack or hear from anyone who thinks they can help use to identify the offender.'

Anyone with information is being asked to contact the CID team on Swansea 6835190.

2 Now look at the report again and put these features in the order they appear in the text. (Write 1 – 6)

a) description of the robber
b) headline
c) appeal for witnesses

d) general information about the crime
e) what actually happened
f) what the police have done

3 If you have completed exercise 2 correctly you should now know that newspaper reports of this kind are often organised as follows:

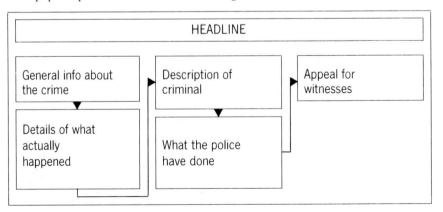

HEADLINE

General info about the crime → Description of criminal → Appeal for witnesses

Details of what actually happened   What the police have done

Writing a report

4.1 Giving general information and supporting details

The purpose of a headline is to attract the reader's attention. The purpose of the first paragraph is to give a general summary of the main points in the report so that readers who are not interested in the detail can stop after the first paragraph.

a) To see if this is true, look at these headlines and first paragraphs. Do they contain a summary of the main points?

Hitch in women's pay claim hearing

A BERKSHIRE industrial tribunal hearing a pay claim by six women cleaners has been stopped on a point of law.

Scientist missing

A HELICOPTER search was due to be launched today for a Thames Valley scientist who vanished on Monday.

Martina crashes

CHRIS EVERT triumphed 6-2 7-5 over Wimbledon Champion Martina Navratilova in their Australian Open semi-final clash in Melbourne today.

Reading Evening Post, 22/1/88.

b) *Task 1*

Using the information below, write two short introductory paragraphs for a report with the headline *SNAKE FOUND ON PLANE*. The first paragraph should provide a summary while the second should give some details.

> Snake / plane / Heathrow Airport / yesterday. Plane / Thailand / about 6 feet long / not dangerous / found by cleaner

c) *Task 2*

Now write two paragraphs in the same way about this information. The headline this time is *WOMAN FINDS £5,000*.

> Woman / bag / £5,000 / outside house / yesterday. The bag / black / leather / on her doorstep / 9 o'clock in the morning.

4.2 Describing people

Look back at the newspaper report in exercise 1. The report describes:

- the approximate **age** of the man
- what the man looked like
- what the man was wearing

Task 3

Finish these sentences with information given about a woman in the box below.

The woman was _____

She was wearing _____

- about 25–30
- tall, blonde long hair overweight
- jeans, black leather jacket white scarf

JIM BASHES BULLY BOYS

SUPER SAVER

Steve sick at softies

Bros beat Beeb boob

MARKED MAN

Charlie cheer

★ CHARLIE NICHOLAS scored his first goal for Aberdeen yesterday, but it came in the shock 2-1 defeat against Motherwell and strengthened Celtic's position at the top of the Scottish premier division. Rangers defeated Falkirk 3-1 in front of a 41,088 crowd.

LUCKY LEAP

A FAMILY of four escaped by climbing out of a bedroom window when fire in a foam-stuffed sofa filled their home with smoke near Chard, Somerset.

STU'S A SAVER

Chris cross

★ STEFFI GRAF, of West Germany, beat veteran American Chris Evert 6-1, 7-6 to win the women's open title at the Australian tennis championships in Melbourne yesterday. Evert complained that closing the roof over the centre court because of rain, upset her concentration.

4.3 Writing headlines

There are two main kinds of headline, both designed to catch the reader's attention.

a) headlines that primarily give **information**
b) headlines that are interesting because of some surprising use of language

Look back at the headlines in exercise 4.1. These clearly give information. Compare them with those on page 48.

Headlines of type a) (in exercise 4.1) are common in the more serious 'quality' newspapers, while type b) headlines (see exercise 4.3) are more common in the 'popular' press

Notice how type b) headlines are full of **alliteration** – that is, words that begin with the same letter

Task 4

Look at these first paragraphs of articles. Work with your partner and try to come up with type b) headlines. See if you can begin every word with the same letter!

A	*B*	*C*
ROMEO Colin Williams fell head over heels for his sweetheart — and ended up in hospital. He plunged 20 feet from a lovers' bridge into a raging river.	THE future looks bleak for Britain's smokers. Three out of four bosses are ready to ban the habit at work and already 62 per cent have imposed a partial block.	SCHOOLGIRL Sarah Wright clung to life in an air bubble — trapped upside down in a car which had plunged into a ditch filled with water.
Today, 17/12/87.	*Mirror, 29/12/87.*	*Sunday Mirror, 24/1/88.*

Writing task

5 Now write a report *either* of an incident that you know about *or* use the information below.

Information

Incident
- Attack on woman (18)
- 12.25 a.m. South Street, Birmingham
- Woman was punched and threatened with a knife

Attacker
- man, white, 20–25, clean-shaven, medium height, short brown hair
- wearing denim jacket, grey trousers

After writing

6 a) Go through the checklist in Unit 3 and try to improve what you have written.
b) Exchange texts with your partner and comment on his/her text.
c) Compare your text with the one suggested in the Key.

Extension task

Find a report in a newspaper from your country – and in your language – and rewrite it according to the model shown in exercise 3.

Writing a Biography

A written biography can either be a whole book or a short report which summarises the main events in the life of an important person. This unit deals with the sort of biographies you can find in encyclopaedias, text books and newspapers.

Discussion

1 What do you think a biography should contain? Work with your partner to fill in the table below.

INFORMATION	YES	NO	INFORMATION	YES	NO
Name			Physical description		
Achievements			Failures		
Education			Beliefs		
Detailed description of family			Date and place of birth		
Details of salary			Reasons for fame		
Details of personal possessions			Dates of important events in his/her life		

2 Now look at these notes about Willy Brandt. Check to see which information from the list above is included.

BRANDT Willy (Herbert Ernst Karl Frahm) (1913–   )

1913	Born in Lubeck, Germany
1932	Started work as apprentice shipbuilder
1933	Emigrated to Norway; changed his name; took Norwegian citizenship; studied at and graduated from University of Oslo
1940/45	Active in Norwegian and German resistance movements
1945	Returned to Berlin
1947	Resumed German citizenship
1949	Elected to West German Assembly as Social Democratic Party (SPD) member for Berlin
1957/66	Mayor of West Berlin
1964	Appointed Chairman of SPD
1966	Became Minister of Foreign Affairs and Vice-Chancellor
1969	Elected Chancellor
1971	Awarded Nobel Peace Prize
1974	Resigned as Chancellor after personal aide exposed as East German spy
1979/83	Member of European Parliament Chairman of Brandt Commission – produced report on state of world economy in 1980
Summary	Will be remembered for his efforts to reduce political tensions between Eastern and Western bloc countries by encouraging joint cooperation projects

Organising writing

3 The text below is a biography of Willy Brandt written from the notes above. However, the paragraphs in the biography are in the wrong order. Biographies are usually written in a strict **time** order. That is, early events in the person's life are mentioned before events which occurred later.

a) Underline the main words, phrases and dates in the paragraphs which refer to **time** and **sequence** and help you to put the paragraphs in the right order.
b) Write the numbers 1 – 6 against the paragraphs to indicate the order you think they should be in.

BRANDT Willy (Herbert Ernst Karl Frahm) (1913–   )

i) Three years later, in 1969, he was elected Chancellor and received the Nobel Peace Prize in 1971. However, he was forced to resign in 1974 after a personal aide was found to be an East German spy. ☐

ii) In 1933 he emigrated to Norway where he changed his name to Willy Brandt and took Norwegian citizenship. During his stay in Norway he graduated from the University of Oslo and became active in Norwegian and German resistance groups. At the end of the war he returned to West Germany and resumed his German citizenship. ☐

iii) From 1979 to 1983 he served as a member of the European Parliament. His most well-known work during this period was as Chairman of the Brandt Commission which produced an important report on the state of the world economy. ☐

iv) Willy Brandt will be remembered for his efforts to reduce political tensions between Western and Eastern bloc countries by promoting joint cooperation projects. ☐

v) Herbert Frahm was born in Lubeck, Germany in 1913. He went to school there and in 1932 began work as an apprentice shipbuilder. ☐

vi) His political career began four years after returning from Norway when he was elected to the West German Assembly as the Social Democratic Party (SPD) member for Berlin. He served as Mayor of West Berlin for eleven years from 1957, and in 1964 was elected Chairman of the SPD. He became Minister of Foreign Affairs and Vice-Chancellor in 1966. ☐

Organising a biography into paragraphs

4 When you have re-ordered the paragraphs in exercise 3, study them again. You will notice that the writer has chosen to organise the text into paragraphs which deal with particular periods of time. This is a useful way to group sentences in this kind of text. Make notes below about the periods of time covered by each of the first five paragraphs in the re-ordered text. The first one is done for you.

PARAGRAPH 1 PARAGRAPH 2 PARAGRAPH 3 PARAGRAPH 4 PARAGRAPH 5	*The period from his birth until he began work.*

Writing longer sentences

5 You have seen one way of organising sentences into paragraphs. It is also important to be able to write sentences that contain more than one idea. Look at these pairs of sentences on the left and one way of combining them to form the longer sentences on the right. The words in italics on the right replace certain words from the pairs of sentences on the left. Find these words and underline them.

a) In 1933 he emigrated to Norway. In Norway he changed his name to Willy Brandt.

In 1933 he emigrated to Norway *where* he changed his name to Willy Brandt.

b) His most well-known work during this period was as Chairman of the Brandt Commission. The Commission produced an important report on the state of the world economy.

His most well-known work during this period was as Chairman of the Brandt Commission *which* produced an important report on the state of the world economy.

c) His political career began four years after returning from Norway. At that time he was elected to the West German Assembly as the SPD member for Berlin.

His political career began four years after returning from Norway *when* he was elected to the West German Assembly as the SPD member for Berlin.

Now fill in the gaps in these sentences with *which*, *where*, *when* or *who*.

d) She was born in Paris _____ she lived until she was twenty.

e) She lived in a house _____ was destroyed by fire.

f) She travelled with her father _____ was a government official.

g) She became well-known in the sixties _____ she began to appear on television.

A model biography

6 You are now familiar with one way of organising a biography.

Title: Full name (with dates)

Where and when was he/she born and brought up?

What were the main events and achievements in his/her life?
- period 1
- period 2
- period 3

Summary: What will he/she be remembered for?

Writing task

7 Write a short biography of between 150–180 words of the kind you would expect to find in an encyclopaedia. *Either* research a character you are particularly interested in *or* use the notes below as the basis for your biography. Whichever you decide, organise your text as shown above.

KENNEDY John F (1917–63)

1917	Born Brookline, Massachusetts USA
	Educated at Harvard
World War 2	Served in Navy
1946	Elected to House of Representatives
1952	Elected to Senate
1960	Elected President of USA (Democrat). Defeated Nixon (Republican). Became first Catholic president and youngest president (44 years old)
1960/63	Established Peace Corps (Organisation for sending young volunteers to work overseas)
	Increased finance available for space programme
	Introduced Civil Rights Bill. Racial discrimination and segregation illegal
	Took US through Cuban missile crisis
1963	Shot dead in Dallas, Texas by Lee Harvey Oswald
Summary	Will be remembered for his youthful idealism, support of civil rights and untimely death

After writing

8 After writing your first draft refer to the checklist on page 20. Then work through your text again to improve it.

When you are satisfied with your final text, compare what you have written with the suggested version in the Key.

Extension tasks

9 a) Find a biography in an encyclopaedia written in your own language. Compare its organisation with the model given in this unit.

b) If you used the notes on John F Kennedy to write your biography, now try writing one about someone you are particularly interested in. It may be a politician, but how about a sports personality, a musician, an actor?

Writing a Report Describing Change

In the last thirty years or so there have been significant changes in the way people live. These changes in lifestyles have been reflected in the way cities, towns and villages have developed.

Discussion

1 Think about the place where you live. What major changes have occurred in your lifetime? Make a list with your partner of all the changes you can think of. Here are some questions to help you.

- Have any big new roads been built?
- Have any large buildings been pulled down?
- Has your town got bigger or smaller?
- Has there been any change in the type of industry?
- Have any new public buildings been put up – for example, sports centres, swimming pools.
- Are shops bigger than they were in the past?
- Have any schools closed down or been built?

When you have made your list, compare what you have written with the changes shown in the maps below.

Collecting information

2 Look at these two maps. They show the town of Windham in 1960 and today. Work with your partner and decide how the town has changed. Then fill in the gaps in the grid below.

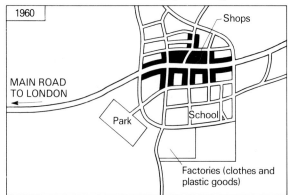

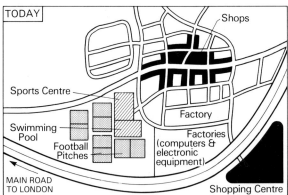

WINDHAM IN 1960	WINDHAM TODAY
Main road to London passes through the town centre	Motorway to London bypasses the town
All shops are in the town centre	
The park is the only leisure facility	
	Children have to travel to next town to attend secondary school
	Factories produce electronic components and computer equipment

3 Read this report of the changes in Windham between 1960 and today. Fill in the gaps with information from exercise 2.

Changes in Windham over the Last Thirty Years

Windham has changed a great deal over the last thirty years or so as the town has developed to meet the changing needs of the people who live there. The
5 volume of traffic has of course increased considerably and the work and leisure activities of its inhabitants have altered.

In the sixties the High Street, which was also part of the _____ road to London was a busy street and the most _____ shopping area. Now,
10 however, the new _____ to London bypasses the _____ and most people do their shopping at the huge new _____ which has opened quite close to it.

15 Windham has far better leisure _____ than it had in 1960. There used to be just one small _____ on the outskirts of the town but now there is a sports centre with a large
20 _____ _____ as well as a number of football _____.

The secondary school has been pulled down and now children have to _____ to the next town ten miles away.

25 Industrial activity has also _____ significantly. The factories that used to produce clothes and plastic goods have been demolished and replaced by new ones producing _____ and
30 _____.

---

4 Now study the passage on the left again and the functions of each paragraph shown below. Then answer the questions. The first one is done for you.

PARAGRAPH 1 General introductory sentence introducing main topics.

What are the main topics?

> Traffic, work and leisure activities

PARAGRAPH 2 Examples of change.

What two examples are given?

> EXAMPLE 1
>
> EXAMPLE 2

PARAGRAPH 3 Example of change. General sentence followed by detail.

What example is given?

> EXAMPLE 3

PARAGRAPH 4 Example of change.

What example is given?

> EXAMPLE 4

PARAGRAPH 5 Example of change. General sentence followed by detail.

What example is given?

> EXAMPLE 5

Organising a paragraph

5 As you can see from exercise 4, the report on Windham begins with a **general** introductory sentence which introduces the main areas of change that the writer is going to deal with, and the remaining paragraphs give **particular examples** of change. This **General-Particular** pattern is a very useful way to organise a report of any kind. If you look carefully at paragraphs 3 and 5 you can see that the **General-Particular** pattern is useful for organising **within paragraphs** as well.

Study the pairs of sentences below and decide whether they are **General** (G) statements or **Particular** (P) statements. Write G or P after each one.

a) i) Agricultural land is disappearing fast. (   )
   ii) There is a housing estate where Bridge Farm used to be. (   )
b) i) The village shop has closed and a new supermarket has been built. (   )
   ii) People no longer want to shop in the traditional way. (   )
c) i) The town centre has changed. (   )
   ii) Blocks of flats have replaced the rows of houses that used to line the High Street. (   )

Vocabulary development

6 Here are some verbs which are useful for writing about changes.

widen	enlarge	develop	improve	rebuild	pull down	put up

Look at the pictures below and use these words to write sentences similar to the example using information from the pictures.

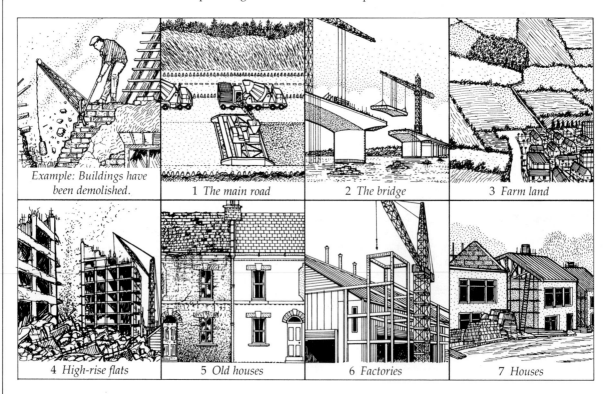

Example: Buildings have been demolished.

1 *The main road*

2 *The bridge*

3 *Farm land*

4 *High-rise flats*

5 *Old houses*

6 *Factories*

7 *Houses*

Writing task

7 *Either* take changes in your own village, town or city as the basis for exercises a) and b) below *or* use these two maps of the village of Morley.

a) Make a list of the changes.

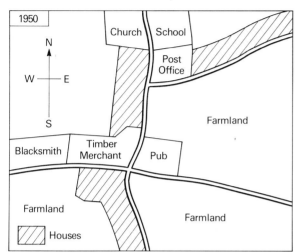
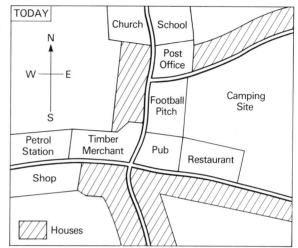

b) Write a report describing the changes using the guidelines below.

- Group the changes you have listed in exercise a) into three or four main categories – for example: leisure facilities, shopping facilities.
- Paragraph 1 should include a general introductory sentence which mentions the extent of and the main kinds of change.
- The remaining paragraphs should each focus on one of these main areas of change and include particular examples. Remember to use the **General–Particular** pattern. (See exercise 5: Organising a paragraph.)
- Try to use the new words from exercise 6.
- Look carefully at the verb tenses used in the report on Windham. Try to include:
  - *USED TO* (e.g. the High Street . . . *used to be* a busy street)
  - *PRESENT PERFECT* (e.g. *ACTIVE* Windham *has changed* a great deal)
    (e.g. *PASSIVE* The secondary school *has been pulled down*)

After writing

8 a) Try to improve your text. Use the checklist in Unit 3 to help you.
  b) Exchange texts with your partner and use the same checklist to comment upon his/her text.
  c) Compare your text with the one suggested in the Key.

Extension task

9 The reports in this unit are written from a **neutral** point of view – that is, they describe changes without the writer stating any **opinions**. Now write your report again from the point of view of someone who is **angry** about what has happened.

Reporting the Results of a Survey

This newspaper article reports the results of a recent survey which looked at the different sorts of jobs men and women do in the home.

Men about the house: Do they pull their weight?

HOW much help around the house can you expect from your man in 1988?

Less than five per cent of husbands, it seems, regularly share the major chores around the house, even if their partners have full or part-time jobs.

For all the talk about liberation of the sexes, it will still be the man who comes home from the pub in 1988 to find his meal in the oven and the house spick and span.

Indeed, the latest reports on the subject confirm what many wives have long expected — that a woman's work in 1988 will never be done...

Says Melanie Harwood, editor of a survey called Inside the Family: "Despite important social changes, particularly greater female employment, it will still be the women in families who will undertake the great bulk of housework, cooking, child care and — increasingly — the looking after of elderly relatives."

Breadwinners

The report is published by the Family Policy Studies Centre, whose director, Malcolm Wicks, says: "Life inside the family in 1988 will still be very different for men and women.

"Women have become workers and second breadwinners, but their traditional tasks — housework and care — are not shared more equally with men."

Take, for instance, the plight of a housewife who has a part-time job. According to research, she will be getting a raw deal in the coming year.

Three-quarters of these women will still have to cook the evening meal, nearly all of them (95 per cent) will do the washing and ironing, 83 per cent will do the cleaning, and 64 per cent will do all the household shopping in 1988.

"Full-time female workers will have an average of seven hours free time for each weekend day, against 10 hours for male full-time workers."

And how women get this time off is something of a mystery — surveys show that mothers will do no less than 87 per cent of the 50 or so hours a week involved in looking after small children.

Repetitive

As the Family Policy Studies Centre says: "Where fathers are involved with child care, this is mainly with the more enjoyable aspects like play and outings — while mothers are more involved with routine and repetitive daily tasks such as feeding, dressing and bathing."

And Inside the Family researchers add: "Typically, little practical support is provided by husbands if there are elderly relatives to be looked after — 85 per cent of the work is done by the housewife.

So just how will husbands spend their time at home in 1988?

"They will involve themselves with household repairs," says the Family Policy Studies Centre, adding that in at least three-quarters of households, hubby is in charge of the screwdriver.

Discussion

1 Look at the headline and the picture.

a) What do you expect the article to be about?
b) What do you think 'pull their weight' means?
c) What do you think the general results of the survey might be?

Collecting information

2 Now read the first column of the article to find this information:

a) The survey is called ' _____

b) The report was published by

_____

c) The year the survey refers to is _____

3 Now read the remainder of the article quickly and fill in the grids on the page opposite. Don't try to understand all the words in the article. Search **only** for the information you need.

Household tasks performed mainly by women

TASK	WOMAN WITH PART-TIME JOB	
Cook evening meal	**75%**	
Do washing and ironing	a)	83 95
Do cleaning	b)	64 83
Do household shopping	c)	85 64
Look after elderly relatives	d)	85
Look after children	e)	87 of the time

Household tasks performed by men

Organising information

4 Look at this report which contains a summary of the main points in the article which you identified in exercise 3. Label each paragraph with one of the following descriptions:

- What men do at home
- What women do at home
- Summary of main conclusions

Inside the Family

A report published by the Family Policy Studies Unit in 1988 called *Inside the Family* suggests that there has been little change in the kinds of tasks carried out by men and women in the home – even in homes where the wife has a job.

5   75% of women with a part-time job still cook the evening meal regularly while 95% take care of all the washing and ironing. Husbands are involved in cleaning in only 17% of the households investigated although more – 36% – are prepared to do the household shopping. The care of elderly relatives and

10   children are also still mainly tasks carried out by women; 85% take responsibility for elderly relatives while 87% of the time spent looking after children is put in by mothers.

   The little time that men spend with children usually involves the more enjoyable aspects of child care such as play and

15   outings. Men also use their time at home on household repairs.

Organising the report

5.1 Writing an introductory paragraph

The introductory paragraph performs two functions. It:

- gives details of the publisher, title and date of the survey
- draws a general conclusion about the findings

Look at the details in the box below. Write an introductory paragraph of two sentences which contains all the information given.

PUBLISHER Schools Council
TITLE Microcomputers in Secondary Schools
YEAR 1988
MAIN FINDINGS
Majority of children believe that their writing has improved by working with word processors

5.2 Presenting a list in readable prose

The other two paragraphs in the summary report in exercise 4 above consist entirely of the detailed findings of the tasks men and women perform. Read the second paragraph in exercise 4 again and compare it with this:

> 75% of women cook the evening meal, 95% do the washing and ironing, 83% do the cleaning, 64% do the household shopping, 85% look after elderly relatives and look after children for 87% of the time.

The text in exercise 4 makes much better reading because it divides up the long list of figures and the structure of the sentences is **varied**.

Look now at these two pieces of information:

> - 75% of women cook the evening meal
> - 95% of women do the washing and ironing

Use this information to complete the sentences below:

a) 75% _____ while 95%

_____

b) The evening meal is _____

while the washing _____

c) Only 5% of men _____

but _____

_____

6 Look at this newspaper report of a different survey on lifestyles in Britain. Find the information needed to complete the sentences and fill in the grid on the next page.

Britain turns into nation of long-lived and languid fat cats

By Peter Murtagh

People in Britain are living longer and are better off, with the result that more and more money is being spent on consumer goods, according to the latest profile of the nation, Britain 1988, a government publication out today.

But while people in general appear to be healthier and wealthier, an analysis of leisure activities suggests they are also lazier. By far the most popular pastime is watching television, with 98 per cent of homes having at least one set and over a third having a video recorder. The average person over the age of four watches about 27 hours of television a week.

Other pastimes include listening to music, DIY, gardening, sports (walking and swimming are favourites), visiting friends or going out for a meal. The 56.8 million people of England, Scotland, Wales and Northern Ireland possess an estimated 12 million household pets.

Sixty nine per cent of homes now have central heating, 81 per cent have washing machines, 95 per cent refrigerators, 81 per cent telephones and 62 per cent of people own a car. Britons are also taking more foreign holidays. United Kingdom residents took over 17 million holidays overseas in 1986, compared with 15.75 million in 1985, and the most popular destinations were unchanged — Spain, France and Greece.

More people are eating meals out and as lifestyles have changed, the consumption of take-away meals, convenience foods and so-called fast food has also risen. Over the past 25 years, consumption of poultry, instant coffee, processed foods, fruit and vegetables has risen while home consumption of beef, veal, mutton, lamb, bread, potatoes, butter, sugar and tea has fallen.

Alcohol consumption is continuing its rise since the 1950s but the type of drinks taken has changed. Beer remains the most popular, but lager now accounts for more than half of beer sales and there has been a switch from whisky and gin to other spirits.

And those of us who survive and prosper can expect to live to the age of 71 for men and 77 for women — a year longer than in 1985.

Britain 1988 — an official handbook, HMSO £12.95.

a)

PUBLISHER		TITLE
MAIN CONCLUSIONS		

b) *Indications of wealth (percentage)*

HOMES WITH:

TELEVISIONS	**98%**	VIDEO		WASHING MACHINES
CENTRAL HEATING		REFRIGERATORS	**95%**	TELEPHONES

PEOPLE WITH CARS

c) *Some information on leisure time*

PEOPLE TAKING HOLIDAYS ABROAD IN 1986	
ALCOHOL CONSUMPTION	**continuing to rise**

d) *Life expectancy*

WOMEN	MEN

Writing task

7 Now use the information in the grids above to help you write a summary report entitled *Living in Britain*. Use this model to help you.

PARAGRAPH 1	Information about publisher, title of survey and main conclusions

PARAGRAPH 2	What most houses in Britain have

PARAGRAPH 3	Some facts about British leisure habits

PARAGRAPH 4	Life expectancy of men and women in 1988

After writing

8 a) Follow the procedures in the checklist in Unit 3.
   b) Exchange texts with your partner and check his/her text against the same checklist.
   c) Compare your text with the one suggested in the Key.

Extension task

9 Why not carry out your own survey on one of the subjects in this unit? Write a short report of your findings.

Creating a Mood: Telling a Story

Telling a story

1 When we tell stories, whether in speech or writing, there is certain information we usually want to give to the listener/reader. This may include information about:

- who is involved in the story: the **participants**
- where the events in the story take place: the **location**
- the circumstances in which the story takes place (the time; what the participants were doing/feeling at the beginning of the story; details about the surroundings/weather etc): the **setting**
- the main things that happen: the **events**
- what happens at the end: the **outcome**

Read the story entitled *Bird* and try to complete the grid below.

PARTICIPANTS	LOCATION	SETTING	EVENTS	OUTCOME

Bird

I was with my friend Patrick in northern Norway up in the Arctic Circle hitchhiking south from Hammerfest. We'd been trying to get a lift all morning but with no success. There was very little traffic – perhaps one or two cars every fifteen
5 minutes. It was midday and we'd been walking for hours following the empty road as it wound along the coast in and out of the fjords. But we didn't mind. It was a beautiful day – crisp and clear. The only sound was our voices which echoed back at us from the folds of the mountains as we talked. The air
10 was still and the sea was calm.
   Suddenly from the corner of my eye I noticed a large black shape swooping towards me out of the silent sky. Then a long ghostly scream . . . AIEEEEE . . . I ducked instinctively just in time as a huge bird rushed past my ears talons reaching out
15 wildly. I turned quickly and watched it soar up into the empty sky and come to rest high above us on a nearby peak. It stood silhouetted against the skyline, screaming bitterly, the harsh sound reverberating eerily in the stillness. We hurried on, hearts pounding, until the screaming stopped and silence
20 descended again.

Looking at words

2.1 Describing the setting

In this short narrative the writer has given a lot of information about the **setting**. We know **where** the events took place, but more importantly he has tried to paint a picture of the way he **felt** by telling us about the weather, the quietness, the lack of movement. Look at the first paragraph of *Bird* again and write down all the words he uses to help us imagine the setting:

2.2 Describing the events

In this story, the writer describes an event which is frightening because of its suddenness and its contrast with the setting. From the *stillness* and *calm* comes a terrifying object. Read the second paragraph of *Bird* again and write down all the words the writer uses to describe the bird and the bird's action:

Getting at the bare facts

3 The sentences below contain the bare facts of the story, leaving out all the descriptive features. Rearrange them into an acceptable order. Write 1 – 7 next to each sentence.

a) A bird attacked me.
b) We were walking along the road.
c) It screamed until we were some distance away.
d) I ducked. The bird just missed me.
e) I was hitchhiking with a friend in northern Norway.
f) The bird flew to a peak above us.
g) We hurried away with hearts pounding.

Organising a story

4 A useful pattern for organising stories is:

SITUATION (Setting/location/participants)
PROBLEM (Usually an event)
RESPONSE TO PROBLEM (Event)
FOLLOW-UP (Outcome)

a) Look back at the bare facts of the story in exercise 3 and label each of the sentences. Some labels will apply to more than one sentence.

b) To show you how common this pattern is for organising stories, look at the extract below which is taken from *Beano* a children's comic. Use the labels above to mark each part of the story.

i) What's the situation?
ii) What's the **first** problem?
iii) What is the boy's response (What does he do)?
iv) What's the second problem?
v) What's the follow-up or outcome?

5 Imagine you are on holiday with a friend. You are at the seaside. It's a beautiful sunny day. You decide to take out a boat. You and your friend lie down to sunbathe and the gentle movements of the waves rock you to sleep. You are woken up by rain on your face and a sudden movement of the boat. You realise you are a long way from the beach and that a storm is beginning to blow. You try to get back to the beach but the sea becomes rough. You are terrified. After half an hour you are rescued by a lifeboat.

Write an essay of about 200 words telling the story from your point of view. Write in the **past tense** and try to describe the **contrast** between when you first took the boat out and the time when the storm was raging. Try to paint a picture for your reader of how it was during the half hour of the storm.

a) Use this grid to help you plan what you are going to write.

SITUATION	PROBLEM	RESPONSE	FOLLOW-UP

b) Using a dictionary and/or a thesaurus write down all the words you can think of that you might use to describe what you were feeling and what was happening i) before the storm ii) during the storm. Use this grid. Some words are given to get you started.

i) BEFORE THE STORM	ii) DURING THE STORM
ADJECTIVES calm, cloudless, clear, happy, relaxed	black, overcast, terrified
VERBS relax, enjoy	shake, toss, throw, whip, rage

6 a) Go through the procedures in the checklist in Unit 3 to try to improve what you have written.
  b) Exchange texts with your partner and use the checklist to comment on his/her text.
  c) Compare your text with the one suggested in the Key.

7 We have all been frightened at some time by something that has happened to us. Think of an event in your life and write a short essay describing what happened and how you felt.

UNIT 15 | Writing an Essay: Approaching the Task

1 Below are some opinions expressed by different people. Read them carefully and see if you can decide what kind of person might have said each. Work with your partner and make notes about the probable **Sex**, **Age** and **Occupation** of the person. Try to match each opinion with one of the photographs below.

A Woman's Place . . .

a) I think everyone has a right to a career. Just because men are incapable of bearing children it doesn't mean that women have to sacrifice themselves to life as a housewife.

b) Throughout history women have looked after the home and the children. Any other arrangement is unnatural.

c) There's nothing wrong with being a housewife. It's a very fulfilling way to spend one's life.

d) It's unfair that in some couples both people work while in others both are unemployed. I think that in any family unit one parent should stay at home with the children and one should work, and I don't think it matters which is which.

e) The unemployment problem would be solved overnight if women were not allowed to work.

f) In my opinion women aren't as competitive as men, and that's the main reason why men will always have the top jobs.

g) What's the point of spending years training a woman who is probably going to give up her job to have children. It's a complete waste of resources.

h) Men should stay at home and look after the children while women go out to work. Why not? Marriage is supposed to be a partnership isn't it?

i) It is obvious that it is a couple's responsibility to sort out how their children are going to be cared for. There is no harm in employing a childminder to look after children. Indeed, I think children can be better brought up by a good childminder than by their own parents.

1) 2) 3) 4) 5) 6) 7) 8) 9)

What do you think of the opinions expressed on the opposite page? Do you agree/disagree? Did you find it easy to match the pictures with the points of view? What does this tell you about yourself and your own prejudices? What made you answer the questions in the way you did? Is it the age of the person? Is it the clothes he or she is wearing? Is it right and correct to believe that we can tell what a person's opinions will be by their **age**, **sex**, **occupation** and the **clothes** they wear?

Writing an essay

2.1 Step 1 Analysing the question

Different people approach an essay writing task in different ways. A good way to begin is by **analysing the question** to make sure you understand exactly what you have to do. Look at this essay question:

Women should stay at home and look after their children rather than go out to work. Discuss.

Essay titles can be analysed from **three** points of view:

THE TOPIC	THE FOCUS	THE COMMENT
The general subject	The particular part of the subject you are asked to concentrate on	Usually a verb which tells you what action you have to take – Define; Describe

Now analyse these titles in the same way:

	TOPIC	FOCUS	COMMENT	ESSAY TITLES
1				Describe the effect of computers on life in the twentieth century
2				Summarise the main arguments for and against the use of animals in medical research

2.2 Step 2 Brainstorming

After analysing the essay title, the next step is to 'brainstorm' as many points as you can think of to do with the **focus** of the essay. For effective brainstorming:

- work with a friend or a small group
- decide on one person to make a list of the group's ideas
- let your mind wander freely . . . think of anything you can that is relevant to the focus of the essay – however outrageous!
- the person making notes writes down **all** the ideas that the group comes up with in the order that they occur. **Don't** try to organise them in any way yet.
- take between 3 – 5 minutes. No more!

Task 1

Following the procedure above, brainstorm the essay title: *Women should stay at home and look after their children rather than go out to work. Discuss.* Write your points on a clean piece of paper.

2.3 Step 3 Organising your ideas

When you have brainstormed a topic you will have a random list of ideas. The next step is to put together ideas which are similar in some way and then to develop a plan for writing. You are likely to have some ideas that are not relevant at all. Get rid of these at this stage.

Below is a list of ideas that arose from a brainstorming session on the topic of *The pressures of examinations*. This list was then organised by giving linked ideas the same number. The list was then reordered into a writing plan.

THE PRESSURES OF EXAMINATIONS

lack of knowledge	handwriting	time/speed
feeling sick	parents	spelling
late/getting up	tired	future/job
haven't studied enough	not good enough	nervous
punctuation	failure	

Writing plan

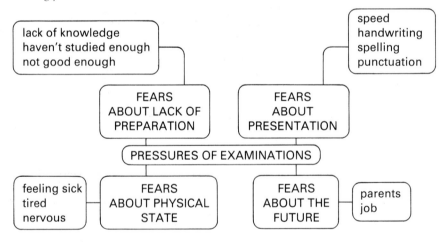

Task 2

Now organise the notes you made in step 2 into main points in the same way.

2.4 Step 4 Writing a first draft

Your first draft should be written quickly from the plan of the main points you identified in step 3. Of course, you will also need to add an introductory sentence and a closing sentence. Do not worry too much about mistakes of grammar, spelling and punctuation. Concentrate on **linking** your ideas well. (See Unit 2 in this book for help with **Linkers**.)

Here are some useful phrases for introducing your opinons. Work with your partner and decide whether they introduce opinions you feel **strongly** about, or ones about which you are **less certain**.

	STRONG	LESS CERTAIN
In my opinion. . . . I think. . . . It is clear that. . . . I believe. . . . It is obvious that. . . . There is no doubt that. . . . It is well-known that. . . .		

2.5 Step 5 Reviewing and editing a first draft

After writing a first draft look carefully at what you have written. Your review should include not only checking for language errors, but also that you have said what you want to say in a logical and persuasive way. Look at this first draft of an essay written by a student. Work through the checklist in Unit 3 and try to identify ways in which it could be improved. Work with your partner and underline language errors then discuss these and other improvements with your teacher.

> Women should stay at home and look after their children rather than go out to work.
> Discuss.
> I am agree with the title - women should stay at home and look after their children.
> There is a lot of reason for my opinion. Firstly, it is nature for a woman to look after children. In the animals world it is always the mother who look after the babies. Humans are not different.
> It is bad for children to stay with another who is not their mother all the time. Soon they will grow up to forget her.
> If a woman do not stay at home she will take a work and this will make problem. She cannot work well if she always worry about the babies.
> Another reason why women should stay in the home is because every country has unemploiement and there is not enough works for all peoples.
> Because of this reasons I believe women should stay at home.

Task 3
Now use the plan you made in step 3 above to write the first draft of an essay of your own on the same topic: *Women should stay at home and look after their children rather than go out to work. Discuss.* Look back at the opinions expressed by the people in exercise 1 if you need help.

After writing

3 a) Follow the procedures in the checklist in Unit 3 and try to improve your first draft.
   b) Exchange texts with your partner and compare his/her text with the same checklist.
   c) Compare your text with the one suggested in the Key.

Extension task

4 Now choose one of the titles below and write an essay. Go through the stages described in exercise 2.
- Young people should be able to marry at the age of 16 without their parents' consent. Discuss.
- All young people should stay at school until the age of 18. Discuss.
- Old people should be looked after by their families not the State. Discuss.

Writing an Essay: Patterns of Organisation

Introduction: Writing essays

1 Essays which contain opinions can be organised in a variety of ways but they normally include the following:

- some background information on the topic
- a section which tells the reader how the essay is organised
- the main arguments for and against
- a conclusion which indicates the writer's opinions

2 Read this essay and draw lines to divide it into four parts which correspond to the descriptions on the right.

SHOULD MILITARY SERVICE BE COMPULSORY?

Military service is compulsory in most countries of the world. In some European countries all citizens are required to spend two years full-time in the army, air force or navy from the age of eighteen and to continue to train on a part-time basis throughout their adult lives to be ready in case of war. In other countries, notably Britain and the United States, military service is not compulsory.

In this essay I intend to look at some of the arguments for and against compulsory military service. First I want to look at the arguments in its favour.

I think there are three main points in support of compulsory military service. Firstly, all countries need a military force. This force defends all the citizens in times of war and therefore all citizens should make some contribution. The second point is a practical one. If a country in unable to attract enough volunteers to the military service then it cannot operate an effective defence. The third and most often mentioned point is that military service is a good discipline for young people - it teaches them practical and social skills and encourages them to take responsibility for themselves and others. A society with compulsory military service is therefore a better society.

The main arguments against are to do with individual freedom. Many people question the value of a young person breaking his or her career or education in order to learn how to kill.

In my opinion, military service should not be compulsory, but some kind of useful social service should be. That is, all young people should be required either to do military service or to work with disadvantaged groups in the community - for example, with those in hospitals, old people's homes, special schools. This experience would be valuable to the community and would also build a sense of responsibility in the individual. However, whether a person chooses military or community service, their commitment should be part-time so that education and career are not interrupted. I also think that all young people should be involved - male and female.

GIVING BACKGROUND INFORMATION

TELLING THE READER HOW THE ESSAY IS ORGANISED

PRESENTING THE ARGUMENTS FOR AND AGAINST

STATING YOUR OPINIONS

What do you think of the writer's arguments? Do you agree? Can you think of any other arguments for or against compulsory military service?

Constructing the essay

3.1 Giving background information

This section of an essay deals with the general topic area and provides information which limits the scope of the topic. In the essay above it answers the question – *What do you mean by military service?* and gives examples from one or two countries.

Look at the texts below which are all possible initial paragraphs for an essay entitled *Should smoking be allowed in public places?* Work with your partner to decide on the following:

Which text is the best opening paragraph? Why? Write your comments on each paragraph in the boxes on the right.

i) In the last ten years people everywhere have become more aware of the dangers of smoking. While it used to be associated with glamour it is now considered a dirty habit. In most countries smokers are separated from non-smokers in public places, while in some countries, particularly the United States, smoking is forbidden in public places such as theatres, cinemas, and trains.

COMMENTS

ii) I think smoking in public places ought to be forbidden because everyone knows that it is harmful to the health and can cause even non-smokers to develop lung cancer and heart disease.

COMMENTS

ii) I don't agree. I think everyone has the right to choose where and when to smoke. To ban smoking in public places is therefore yet another attack on individual freedom. Anyway, where is the proof that 'passive' smoking can lead to lung cancer and heart disease?

COMMENTS

3.2 Stating how the essay is organised

In a short essay this can be done in one or two sentences. Look at the sentences used in the sample essay:

> In this essay I intend to look at the arguments for and against compulsory military service. First I'm *going to deal with arguments in its favour*.

Notice how the words in this part **point forward** to the remainder of the essay.

a) Underline all the words that refer forward to the rest of the essay.
b) *Vocabulary development*
    Using a dictionary or a thesaurus, find words and phrases that can be used to replace these words taken from the paragraph above.

| intend | look at | deal with | arguments |

c) *Task 1*

Now write a similar paragraph which gives the reader information about how you will organise an essay entitled *Should smoking be allowed in public places?* Experiment with the alternative words and phrases you found in exercise b) on page 71.

3.3 Stating the arguments for and against

In this section you are presenting the main arguments. Remember that you are **not** giving your own opinions. A good way to construct this section can be represented like this:

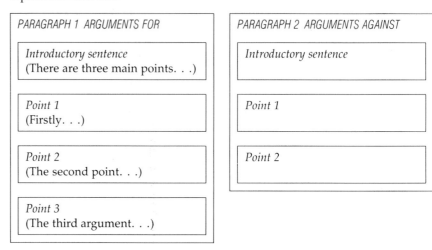

PARAGRAPH 1 ARGUMENTS FOR
Introductory sentence (There are three main points. . .)
Point 1 (Firstly. . .)
Point 2 (The second point. . .)
Point 3 (The third argument. . .)

PARAGRAPH 2 ARGUMENTS AGAINST
Introductory sentence
Point 1
Point 2

a) Now look back at the sample text. Find the introductory sentences and main points and label them.

b) *Task 2*

Look at these arguments **for** and **against** smoking in public places. Use them to write this section of the essay entitled *Should smoking be allowed in public places?* Use the model shown above and add any points you want to include.

FOR

- Everyone has the right to smoke when and where they like
- No proof that 'passive' smoking leads to lung cancer and heart disease

AGAINST

- Smoking is a dirty habit
- Smoking is dangerous – can cause fires
- 'Passive' smoking can cause lung cancer and heart disease
- Non-smokers have the right to be in a smoke-free environment

3.4 Stating your opinions

In this final part of the essay you write about what **you** think. When we give our opinions we introduce our ideas by using words and phrases like this:

In my opinion military service *should* be compulsory.

Look back at the last paragraph of the sample essay in exercise 2 and underline all the words and phrases that show the writer is stating an opinion or thought.

Task 3

Now write a final paragraph for the essay *Should smoking be allowed in public places?* Remember that this paragraph should contain your opinions about the arguments you have presented (without opinion) in exercise 3.3.

After writing

4 a) Go through the checklist in Unit 3 and try to improve what you have written.

b) Exchange texts with your partner and check his/her essay against the same checklist.

c) Compare the texts you produced in exercise 3 with those suggested in the Key.

Writing model

5 In this unit you have worked with the following model for an essay:

> PARAGRAPH 1
> *Giving background information*

> PARAGRAPH 2
> Stating how the essay is *organised*

> PARAGRAPH 3
> Arguments FOR
> • Introductory sentence
> • Point 1
> • Point 2
> • *Point n*

> PARAGRAPH 4
> Arguments AGAINST
> • Introductory sentence
> • Point 1
> • *Point n*

> PARAGRAPH 5
> *Stating your opinions*

Extension task

6 Write an essay of about 200 words on any one of these topics:
• The wearing of school uniform should be compulsory
• The wearing of seat belts in cars should be compulsory
• People who drink alcohol and drive should be sent to prison
• All people should be required by law to have an AIDS test

Answer key

UNIT 1 Thinking about Writing

1 a) I'm afraid I *not can to* come tomorrow. Mistake of grammar and word order. Correct: *I'm afraid I cannot come tomorrow.*

b) *january.* Mistake of punctuation. Correct: January

c) Mistakes of punctuation. Correct: *Are you going home during the summer this year?*

d) Mistake of spelling. Correct: *quiet*

e) Mistake in organisation. Correct: Mrs H E John, 18, Baker Street, London NW1 4NS, England.

2 *LETTERS* Letter B is much better than letter A. Letter A: is too short; comes to the point too quickly; does not explain WHY money is needed; is rude – the writer appears to be commanding rather than asking; has an inappropriate ending – we do not end a letter to a bank manager with 'Love' and we normally sign our name in full.

TELEXES Telex A is much better than telex B. Telex A is brief and contains the information needed and no more. Telex B should NOT have: the full postal address of the person you are sending it to – or your own; unnecessary pleasantries such as 'I hope you are feeling well'; 'yours sincerely' at the end.

3

TEXT	PURPOSE	AUDIENCE	TEXT TYPE
B	Asking for advice	Magazine writer and readers	Letter
C	To interest, inform and appeal for witnesses	Newspaper readers	Newspaper report
D	To give instructions	People who have bought the camera	Instruction manual

UNIT 2 Organising your Writing: Using Linking Words and Phrases

1 The order is: c) b) a) d) e) f) h) g).

2 A few minutes later, after, In August 1975, when, at first, then, finally, by this time, a second time, then.

3 These words and phrases link Cause and Effect/Consequence.

4 The match this afternoon is cancelled (E) because of bad weather. (C)

There has been no rain (C) so the crops can't grow. (E)

People are in danger (E) as a result of radiation leaks from nuclear power stations. (C)

Smoking is dangerous (C) therefore it shouldn't be allowed in public places. (E)

4.1 Once again the rains have failed to come in time to Ethiopia. *As a result the crops planted last year have not grown.* Millions of people are facing starvation. Emergency food and medical supplies are being sent through international relief organisations and stockpiled at ports. However, transportation of these supplies to distant areas remains an almost impossible problem *because of the lack of good roads and the continuing civil war.*

More than fifty per cent of the lorries used in the last relief operation two years ago are damaged beyond repair *so the relief organisations are desperately seeking international help to send in supplies by plane.*

5 a) because as, since   b) consequently, therefore, as a result   c) so   d) as, because, since   e) consequently, therefore, as a result

6 *TIME/SEQUENCE:* Firstly, secondly

COMPARING/CONTRASTING: However, while, whereas, by contrast

GIVING EXAMPLES: for example, such as

EXPLAINING: What I mean by this is. . . .

7.1 a) While 95% of children attend state schools, only 5% attend private schools.   b) George is taller than Peter whereas Peter can run faster than George.

7.3 a) I don't agree that military service teaches a young person useful skills. *For example,* learning how to kill is not a useful skill.   b) I can think of lots of reasons why compulsory military service is a good idea. *For instance,* it allows you to meet people from different backgrounds.   c) If military service is to be compulsory it should be compulsory for everyone. *What I mean by this is* that women should also be obliged to do military service.

UNIT 3 Improving your Writing

1 a) *STUDENT* Before writing: reads question carefully, makes notes on main points to guide reading, discusses essay with a friend. While writing first draft: makes detailed notes then organises them, writes the main part of the essay THEN the conclusion and introduction. After writing first draft: checks main points are there, rereads question, checks that order is logical and argument well-supported, checks spelling and grammar, asks a friend to read it.

BUSINESSPERSON Before writing: thinks about readers. While writing first draft: writes separate sections on word processor then organises them to company guidelines. After writing first draft: prints it then reads it to check organisation, clarity, grammar, spelling and punctuation; asks a colleague to read it through.

NOVELIST Before writing: thinks of a plot and the characters. While writing first draft: thinks a lot about individual words and phrases; redrafts several times. After writing first draft: drafts again and again but leaves spelling, punctuation and typing errors to the proofreader.

b) *STUDENT* Writing for an examiner/supervisor whose reasons are to find out if the writer has worked hard and understands the work done.

BUSINESSPERSON Usually writing to give information to colleagues, (External reports may be for other reasons.) The colleagues are reading to get accurate information quickly.

NOVELIST Novelists write partly for themselves and partly for people who read for pleasure.

3 The address and date are correct. Here is a suggested way of improving the body of the letter:

Dear Sir/Madam,

I attended the evening performance of 'The Boyfriend' last Thursday and unfortunately left my bag on the seat.

The bag is black, made of soft leather and has the initials BJ on the front.

If it has been handed in I would be grateful if you could let me know as soon as possible.

Yours faithfully,

4 (1) became   (2) twice   (3) studied   (4) was not elected
(5) gave birth to   (6) several (a number of, many)
(7) developed

5 My name is Natalie Hirsch. I am twenty years old and I am studying graphic design in my country. One of the things I like most is being with children. If I hadn't studied graphic design I would like to have trained to be a teacher. I enjoy playing with children and think I would enjoy teaching because I have a lot of patience. I would like to get a job in London looking after children. I think it would be a good experience. If I find a job I'll stay here for about three years.

UNIT 4 Writing a Letter to a Friend

1 The phrases you would find are: a) b) d) g) i) j)
2 BEGINNINGS How're things?; I refer to your letter dated July 28th; Thanks for your recent letter; It was so nice to hear from you.
ENDINGS See you soon; Take care; Yours sincerely; Yours faithfully; Look forward to seeing you in August.
3 1a) 2b) 3d) 4c) 5j) 6i) 7g) 8h) 9f) 10e)
4 Suggested answer: (others possible)

> Norregade 77
> 6200 VARDE
> Denmark
>
> 28/10/88
>
> Dear Dick,
>
> It was nice to get your letter. I've been meaning to write to you for a long time, but I'm so bad at keeping in touch.
>
> I'm glad you're enjoying your new job – it sounds exciting! Since I last saw you I've been doing a lot of different things. After I left London I travelled to Paris to meet my cousin, then we went to the South of France to find work for a month picking grapes. It was hard work but the pay was quite good. At the end of September I returned home to start a course in Hotel Management. I'm enjoying it, but I'm looking forward to the Christmas holidays!
>
> What are you doing at Christmas? How about coming to visit us here – there's plenty of room. Think about it and tell me soon.
>
> My mother sends her love. Hope to see you at Christmas.
>
> Take care,
>
> Karsten

5.1 STRONG I'm so grateful; I can't thank you enough.

5.2

GOOD	BAD
great	awful
wonderful	horrible
amazing	terrible
fantastic	disastrous
lovely	appalling
marvellous	depressing
pleasant	
nice	

5.3 Suggested answers:
- *How about* going to France?
- *The best way to* get money quickly is to borrow it from the bank.
- *Why don't you try* the fish?

6 Suggested answer:

> Norregade 77
> 6200 VARDE
> Denmark
>
> 28/11/88
>
> Dear Dick,
>
> Thanks for your replying so quickly to my last letter. I'm so glad you are able to come and stay with us at Christmas.
>
> My holiday doesn't start until December 22, so why don't you plan to come on the 23rd? The best way to come is to take the ferry from Harwich to Esbjerg. I'll pick you up from the ferry. There's no need to bring your car – the ferry ticket for a car is quite expensive.
>
> Although there's not much to do in Varde itself, we could go and visit some friends of mine in Arhus, and spend a few days between Christmas and the New Year in Copenhagen.
>
> Let me know your travel arrangements as soon as you can.
>
> Look forward to seeing you.
>
> Best wishes,
>
> Karsten

UNIT 5 Writing Letters of Complaint

1 1 Your address
2 The date
3 Address of the person you are writing to
4 Dear . . .
5 Main reason for writing
6 Background information 1
7 Complaint
8 Background information 2
9 Request for action
10 Ending
11 Your name

2 a) Address of person you are writing to is placed on the left below your address.
  b) Because she doesn't know the name or sex of the person she is writing to.
  c) The ending depends on the salutation. If you write *Dear Sir* or *Madam* you normally end with *Yours faithfully* or *Yours truly*. If you begin with a name – for example – *Dear Mr Smith* or *Dear Ms Thomas* then you normally end with *Yours sincerely*.
  d) Ms – can be used for any female; does not indicate whether the person is married or unmarried
  Mr – can be used for any male; does not indicate whether the person is married or unmarried
  Miss – indicates an unmarried woman
  Mrs – indicates a married woman

3.1 a) I am writing to complain about a TV I bought from your shop last Thursday.
  b) I am writing to complain about a watch I bought from your shop last Friday.
  c) I am writing to complain about a car I hired from your company last Tuesday.
  d) I am writing to complain about a meal I had in your restaurant last Sunday.

3.2 a) I bought the TV from your shop on Thursday 23rd November. I took it home, but when I turned it on I found it didn't work. I checked the plug but that wasn't the problem.
  b) I hired a car from your company on Tuesday 18th February. I drove to London Airport to catch a plane. Unfortunately, on the way I had a puncture. When I took out the spare wheel I found it was flat. I tried to phone you for over half an hour but there was no answer. As a result, I missed my plane.
  c) When I put the shirt on I discovered it was torn.
  When I took out the spare wheel I found it was flat.
  As soon as I turned it on it started to get hot.
  The first time I wore them the heel fell off.
  d) Suggested answers:
  When I cut the bread I found a large piece of glass inside.
  As soon as I sat on it – it collapsed!

3.3 a)(1) b)(2) c)(1) d)(2) e)(2) f)(1)

3.4 a) *send my money back* – give me a refund
  b) *give me a reduction in the price* – give me a discount
  c) *send me a new one* – give me a replacement
  d) *tell me what happened* – give me an explanation
  e) *say sorry* – give me an apology

4

> 42 Long Road
> Liverpool
>
> 12 February 1988
>
> The Manager
> Savoy Restaurant
> 76 High Street
> Liverpool
>
> Dear Sir/Madam
>
> I am writing to complain about a meal I had in the Savoy Restaurant last Friday evening.
>
> I took a group of business friends to the restaurant because I had heard that the food and the standard of service was excellent.

However, when we arrived at the restaurant we found that no reservation had been made although I had confirmed it by phone the day before. After waiting for a table for over an hour we were kept waiting a further hour before we were served. When the food finally arrived the vegetables were cold and the plates were dirty. When I complained to the waiter he became rude. I was disgusted by the treatment we received and shall certainly never eat there again.

I feel that at the very least you owe my guests and me an apology and await an answer from you.

Yours faithfully

Colin Thomas

5 Suggested answer:

> 24 Albert Road
> Manchester
>
> 15 April 1988
>
> The Manager
> College Bookshop
> 26 Stone Square
> Manchester
>
> Dear Sir/Madam
>
> I am writing to complain about a book I bought in your shop on Saturday morning.
>
> The name of the book was the 'Guide to British Birds'. I was in a hurry so I didn't examine it very carefully before I paid for it. When I got home I sat down to have a look at it and found, to my surprise, that a number of pages were missing.
>
> I enclose the book with a copy of my receipt. Could you please send me a replacement as soon as possible?
>
> Yours faithfully
>
> John Stephenson

6 Suggested answer:

> 25 Hill Close
> Wandsworth
> London
>
> 25/8/88
>
> The Manager
> Pete's Place
> 212 Oxford Street
> London
>
> Dear Sir/Madam
>
> I am writing to complain about a record I bought in your shop last Saturday.
>
> When I got the record home I discovered that it was badly scratched and completely unplayable.

I enclose the record with a copy of my receipt and would be grateful if you could send me either a new record or my money back. I hope to hear from you in the next few days.

Yours faithfully

Andy Jones

UNIT 6 Applying for a Course of Study

3.1

18 Famagusta Street
Nicosia
Cyprus

September 23 1989

The Registrar
University of Gwent
Newtown
Gwent
South Wales

Dear Sir/Madam

I saw your recent advertisement in an Educational Supplement concerning postgraduate courses for overseas students.

I am particularly interested in the MA course in International Studies.

Could you please send me full details and an application form.

Yours faithfully

Stavros Giorgiou

5

25, Rue des Jardins,
47000 Villeneuve,
France

25 October 1989

The Registrar
Regents College
Inner Circle
Regents Park
London NW1 4NS

Dear Sir/Madam

I saw your recent advertisement in the Guardian concerning summer courses at Regents College.

I am particularly interested in the 4-week drama courses.

Could you please send me full details and an application form.

Yours faithfully

6.1 a) block letters   b) surname   c) former
d) mother tongue   e) permanent

6.2 a) Master of Arts   b) Bachelor of Science   c) Bachelor of Music   d) Master of Science   e) Bachelor of Law   f) Master of Business Administration

6.3

University College of Gwent

Registration for a higher degree or research course

SURNAME (Block letters) GIORGIOU	FORMER SURNAME (If applicable) N/A

FIRST NAMES (In full) STAVROS	MARITAL STATUS M = Married S = Single [S]	SEX M = Male F = Female [M]

DATE OF BIRTH 28 7 67 day month year	NATIONALITY CYPRIOT	MOTHER TONGUE GREEK

PERMANENT HOME ADDRESS 18, FAMAGUSTA STREET, NICOSIA, CYPRUS	COUNTRY (If Overseas) OR CYPRUS COUNTY (If U.K.) N/A

Telephone number:

ADDRESS FOR CORRESPONDENCE DURING THIS APPLICATION AS ABOVE Telephone number: N/A	IF YOU HAVE ATTENDED THE SCHOOL BEFORE STATE DATES AND SUBJECT(S) TAKEN I AM INTERESTED IN TAKING THE COURSE BECAUSE I HOPE TO WORK IN THE DIPLOMATIC SERVICE.

COURSE PROPOSED 1. Title of degree: MA 2. Subject: INTERNATIONAL STUDIES 3. Full-time/Part-time: FULL-TIME 4. Starting date: 1990 OCTOBER	REASONS FOR WISHING TO TAKE THE COURSE I WANT TO STUDY IN BRITAIN BECAUSE OF THE QUALITY OF THE COURSES AND BECAUSE I WOULD LIKE TO STUDY THROUGH ENGLISH – THE MAIN LANGUAGE OF DIPLOMACY.

PREVIOUS EDUCATION
(i) Schools attended since age of 11:
INTERNATIONAL SCHOOL, NICOSIA, CYPRUS   GCE A-LEVELS   GEOGRAPHY -B
(ii) School leaving certificate obtained (If GCE Advanced Level, give the grades):   HISTORY – A   ECONOMICS- A

(iii) Universities attended with dates	Degree	Main Subject	Class or Grade	Date
ATHENS UNIVERSITY	BA	BUSINESS ADMINISTRATION	A	1986-89

(iv) University at which you are presently enrolled:	N/A		Date of examination:

UNIT 7 Writing a Personal Description

1 a) doctor; lawyer; teacher; engineer
b) Yes – own comfortable room; all meals provided; generous salary; plenty of time off
c) Age, sex, background, current occupation, experience of looking after children, reasons for wanting the job, level of English, can she drive? what are her interests?

2

GOOD	BAD
honest	lazy
caring	irresponsible
modest	dishonest
conscientious	aggressive
reliable	mean
warm-hearted	cold
hard-working	
kind	

4 I hope to finish next year; and would like to find a job with a large company; my friends tell me I play well but I don't think I'm very good; I feel that I am responsible.

5 The letter is rude, too short, and does not provide enough information.
Here is a suggested improved letter

> My name is Natalia and I come from Madrid in Spain. I've got a brother and sister who are 4 and 6 so I have some experience of looking after children.
>
> I'm a student at Madrid University at the moment and am interested in the job not only because I like looking after children but also because I want to improve my English by living and working in an English environment. I am particularly interested in living in London because I love theatre and opera.
>
> I'd be grateful if you could give me details of the salary and the working hours.

6 Paragraph 1 – c) g)   Paragraph 2 – b) a)
Paragraph 3 – e)   Paragraph 4 – f) d)

UNIT 8 Taking Notes

2 a) Take note *NB*; b) that is *i.e.*; c) for example *e.g.*;
d) namely *viz*; e) compare with *cf*; f) and so on *etc.*;
g) causes →; h) therefore ∴; i) because ∵; j) is not the same as ≠; k) also, and +; l) results from ←; m) is the same as =; n) more than >; o) less than <

3.1 Twenty five per cent of road accidents were caused by drunk drivers in 1986.

3.2 Sixty per cent of British people took holidays abroad in 1988 compared with 42 per cent in 1981. The most popular destinations were in the Mediterranean, for example, Greece, Turkey and Spain.

4 a) Heat → ice to melt
b) Standard of living in Br. today < 10 years ago
c) Computers today used > 10 years ago ∵ cheaper
d) Children learn FL > easily adults. ∴ FL should be taught in primary schools.

5 a) How have computers changed in the last 30 years?
b) What are the advantages of computers? OR What can computers do well?
c) What are the limitations of computers?

6 Notes *A* and *B* summarise the information more clearly than *C*. *A* contains more information than *B*, therefore *A* is the best set of notes.

8

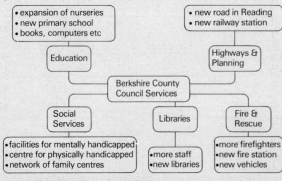

UNIT 9 Writing Instructions

1 a) i) iv) v) iii) ii) vi)
b) i) *first, then* vi) *finally*

c) Sentence i) the acoustic cover
Sentence iii) the ribbon
Sentence vi) the ribbon cassette
d) i) Almost all the verbs are IMPERATIVES (Lift; remove; put etc.). We can make a negative command by putting DON'T in front of these verbs. Thus: *Don't lift the acoustic cover. . .; Don't turn the power switch off.* etc. ii) We understand the READER to be the subject.

2 Suggested answer:
Instructions for British Airways Passengers arriving at London Heathrow Airport
● Follow the ARRIVALS signs
● At Immigration show your passport and health documents
● Next, proceed to the ARRIVALS BAGGAGE RECLAIM AREA. Follow the signs for your flight number
● Check to make sure you collect the right bag
● Next, go to CUSTOMS. Go through the RED channel if you have goods to declare; go through the GREEN channel if you have nothing to declare

3 If oil catches fire in the frying pan. . . . *Turn the cooker off; Put some water on a cloth; Cover the frying pan with the wet cloth; Leave the frying pan for half an hour until it cools down.*

4 b)

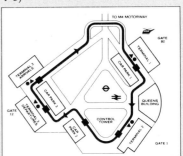

5 Suggested answer:
Turn right out of the station and walk to the end of that street. Then turn right and go under the railway bridge until you come to some traffic lights. At the traffic lights go left. Keep walking past a row of shops until you come to a roundabout just before the river. The White Horse Hotel is on the corner opposite a garage.

UNIT 10 Writing a Newspaper Report

1 Features present: Headline; Information about the kind of crime committed; Details of crime; Description of criminal; Appeal for witnesses

2 The Order is: 1 b) 2 d) 3 e) 4 a) 5 f) 6 c)

4.1 b) Suggested answer:
A large snake was found on a plane at Heathrow Airport yesterday.
The snake, which was brought in on a plane from Thailand, was about six feet long but was not considered to be dangerous. It was found by a cleaner.

4.1 c) A woman found a bag containing £5,000 outside her house yesterday.
The bag was black and made of leather. The woman found it on her doorstep at 9 o'clock yesterday morning.

4.2 Suggested answer:

The woman was *about 25 to 30 years old, and was tall and overweight with long blonde hair.*

She was wearing *jeans, a black leather jacket and a white scarf.*

4.3 Suggested Answers:

A BAN BY BRITAIN'S BOSSES

B LOVER'S LEAP

C SCHOOLGIRL SARAH SAVED!

5 Suggested answer:

MAN ATTACKS GIRL

A girl of 18 was attacked in Birmingham on Saturday night. The attack took place at 12.25 a.m. in South Street. A man punched the girl and threatened her with a knife.

The attacker is described as 20–25 years old, clean-shaven, of medium height and with short brown hair. He was wearing a denim jacket and grey trousers.

Birmingham police would like to speak to anyone who was in the area at the time of the attack.

UNIT *11* Writing a Biography

1 A biography is unlikely to contain the following: detailed description of family; details of salary; detailed physical description; details of failures.

2 The notes on Willy Brandt contain the following: name; date and place of birth; education; dates of important events in his life; achievements; beliefs; reasons for fame

3 a) i) *Three years later . . in 1969 . . in 1971 . . in 1974 . .*
   ii) *In 1933 . . During his stay in Norway . . At the end of the war . .*
   iii) *From 1979 to 1983 . . during this period . .*
   iv) none
   v) *. . in 1913 . . in 1932 . .*
   vi) *. . four years after . . for eleven years, from 1957 . . in 1964 . . in 1966*

   b) The order is: 1 v) 2 ii) 3 vi) 4 i) 5 iii) 6 iv)

4 PARAGRAPH 2 His time in Norway
   PARAGRAPH 3 The beginning of his political career until he became Vice-Chancellor
   PARAGRAPH 4 The period between his election as Chancellor and his resignation
   PARAGRAPH 5 His time in the European Parliament

5 a) *where* replaces *In Norway*
   b) *which* replaces *The Commission*
   c) *when* replaces *at that time*
   d) *where* e) *which* f) *who* g) *when*

7 Suggested answer:

KENNEDY John F (1917–63)
John F Kennedy was born in Brookline, Massachusetts, USA in 1917. He was educated at Harvard and served in the Navy during World War 2.

He entered politics after the end of the war and was elected to the House of Representatives in 1946. Six years later he was elected to the Senate.

In 1960, at the age of 44, he became the youngest ever President of the United States. He defeated Richard Nixon in the election and in doing so, became the first Catholic president.

During his term of office his achievements included establishing the Peace Corps, and introducing the Civil Rights Bill making racial discrimination and segregation

illegal. Under his presidency the US space programme received increased finance. He also guided the US through the Cuban missile crisis.

In 1963, at the age of 46, he was shot dead in Dallas, Texas by Lee Harvey Oswald.

John F Kennedy will be remembered for his youthful idealism, his support of human rights and his untimely death.

UNIT *12* Writing a Report Describing Change

2 (variations are possible)
   1960 – All shops in the town centre; Today – Big new shopping centre near the motorway.
   1960 – The park is the only leisure facility; Today – Large sports centre, swimming pool and football pitches.
   1960 – School in the town; Today – Children have to travel to next town to attend secondary school.
   1960 – Factories produced clothes and plastic goods; Today – Factories produce electronic components and computer equipment.

3 (From paragraph 2)
In the sixties the High Street, which was also part of the *main* road to London, was a busy street and the most *important* shopping area. Now, however, the new *motorway* to London bypasses the *town* and most people do their shopping at the huge new *shopping centre* which has opened quite close to it.

Windham has far better leisure *facilities* than it had in 1960. There used to be just one small *park* on the outskirts of the town, but now there is a sports centre with a large *swimming pool* as well as a number of football *pitches*.

The secondary school has been pulled down and now children have to *travel* to the next town ten miles away.

Industrial activity has also *changed* significantly. The factories that used to produce clothes and plastic goods have been demolished and replaced by new ones producing *electronic components* and *computers*.

4 (variations are possible)
   EXAMPLE 1 motorway has been built
   EXAMPLE 2 the main shopping area has moved from the town centre to the new shopping centre
   EXAMPLE 3 leisure facilities have improved: e.g. sports centre
   EXAMPLE 4 school has been pulled down
   EXAMPLE 5 factories make different products: computers and electronic components

5 a) i) G ii) P b)i) P ii) G c)i) G ii) P

6 Suggested answers:
   1 The main road *has been widened.*
   2 The bridge *has been rebuilt.*
   3 Farm land *has been developed.*
   4 High-rise flats *have been pulled down.*
   5 Old houses *have been improved.*
   6 Factories *have been enlarged.*
   7 Houses *have been put up.*

7 b) Suggested answer:
   Morley has changed a great deal over the last forty years or so as the village has developed to meet the changing needs of the people who live there. The population of the village has increased and more facilities are now available. This has meant some

changes in the use of the surrounding land.

The most obvious change is to do with the buildings. Since 1950 new houses have been built on what used to be farm land opposite the village pub. While most of the traditional buildings – the village school, church and post office remain, some, such as the blacksmith's, have disappeared altogether. The village now has a petrol station, a restaurant and a new shop.

More leisure facilities are also available than in 1950. There is a football pitch between the pub and the post office, and a camping site behind it.

The use of land surrounding the village has altered as the village has grown. The area east of the village used to be farm land but since 1950 it has gradually disappeared to make room for new houses and facilities.

UNIT 13 Reporting the Results of a Survey

2 a) Inside the Family b) Family Policies Study Centre c) 1988

3 a) 95% b) 83% c) 64% d) 85% e) 87%
Household tasks performed by men: enjoyable aspects of looking after children and household repairs

4 PARAGRAPH 1 Summary of main conclusions
PARAGRAPH 2 What women do at home
PARAGRAPH 3 What men do at home

5.1 A report published by the Schools Council in 1988 called 'Microcomputers in Secondary Schools' suggests that the majority of children believe that their writing has improved by working with word processors.

5.2 a) 75% of women cook the evening meal while 95% do the washing and ironing.
  b) The evening meal is cooked by 75% of women while the washing and ironing is done by 95%.
  c) Only 5% of men do the washing and ironing while 25% cook the evening meal.

6 a) Publisher: HMSO. Title: Britain 1988. Main Conclusions: British people are better off in 1988 than ever before.
  b) video: (about) 35% washing machines: 81%
  central heating: 69% telephones: 81% cars: 62%
  c) holidays abroad in 1986: over 17 million
  d) Life expectancy: Men – 71; Women – 77

7 Suggested answer:
A report published by HMSO in 1988 called 'Britain 1988' suggests that British people are better off today than they have ever been.

One way in which life has improved is the extent to which people own various household goods. Almost all households in Britain have a television while over a third have a video recorder. Washing machines are available in 81% of houses and refrigerators in 95%. 69% of homes have central heating while 81% have telephones. Just under two-thirds of British families have a car.

The leisure habits of the British are another measure of wealth. Alcohol consumption continues to rise while more people took holidays abroad in 1986 (17 million) than ever before.

Life expectancy is also increasing. In 1988 men can expect to live to 71 and women to 77.

UNIT 14 Creating a Mood: Telling a Story

1 PARTICIPANTS The writer, Patrick, the bird
LOCATION northern Norway near Hammerfest, on a country road next to the sea
SETTING empty, quiet road, beautiful day, midday, crisp and clear. Calm sea, still air. Walking for hours.
EVENTS 1 Two people walking along the road 2 A bird attacks them 3 The bird returns to a mountain peak
OUTCOME They walk on with the bird screaming behind them.

2.1 little traffic, empty road, wound along the coast, beautiful day, crisp and clear, voices echoed, air was still, sea was calm

2.2 large black shape, swooping, long ghostly scream, huge bird, rushed past, talons reaching out wildly, soar, silhouetted, screaming bitterly, harsh sound reverberating eerily

3 The order is: e) b) a) d) f) g) c)

4 a) SITUATION e) and b) PROBLEM a) RESPONSE d) FOLLOW-UP f) g) and c)
  b) i) Boy in tree looking after baby playing below. Boy falls asleep ii) Boy wakes up to find baby in tree iii) Boy puts baby to sleep on a branch iv) Branch breaks and baby falls v) Baby falls on boy and bounces happily

5 Suggested answer:
SITUATION Sailing with a friend. You sunbathe and both fall asleep. PROBLEM You wake up to find you are a long way from the beach and a storm is beginning to blow. RESPONSE You try to get back to the beach but the sea is rough. FOLLOW-UP You are rescued by a lifeboat.

I was on holiday with my friend Louise on Ios, an island in Greece. It was late September and the weather was wonderful. It was about midday and the sun was streaming down from a cloudless deep blue sky. We decided to take a boat out and drift around sunbathing. It was so relaxing lying in the boat. Although the sun was hot a slight sea breeze blew gusts of cool air over us. The waves lapped gently at the boat and rocked us slowly. I drifted off to sleep with the taste of salt on my lips and the fresh scents of the ocean filling my mind.

A violent lurch of the boat awoke me with a start. Large drops of rain were falling on my face and arms and I shivered at the sudden cold. Louise was sitting up. The sky had turned black and the heavy clouds were low in the sky. I looked towards the beach and to my horror saw that we had drifted far into the open sea.

We dressed quickly and tried to row towards the shore but the sea was so rough that we made little progress. For half an hour we struggled against the raging sea which tossed our boat around as if it were a toy. We were desperate and terrified. We really thought we were going to die.

Then, in the distance, we heard the sound of a motor boat. We held our breath, praying that help was on its way. Slowly out of the rain came a white shape . . . it was the island lifeboat coming to get us! We were so relieved to climb aboard, and so grateful to be saved.

UNIT 15 Writing an Essay: Approaching the Task

2.1 1 TOPIC Computers FOCUS Their effect on life in the twentieth century COMMENT Describe